VORTEX
ARCHITECTURE OF THE CIRCLE

Rizzoli Electa

Philip Jodidio

For a pension fund to be invited to invest in a project with guaranteed returns, such as the Vortex, is an extraordinary opportunity, and will no doubt remain unique in its history.

First of all, the clearly high-cost scheme was bound to a very short timeframe for completion: everything had to be ready by January 2020 to welcome the 1,700 athletes who would be participating at the 2020 Youth Olympic Games (YOG). These athletes would be the first, temporary residents of what can rightly be termed a "village"—an Olympic village in a single building!

Secondly, there was the architectural quality of the project, the originality of which immediately won over the board members who were charged with deciding whether or not to finance this public-private partnership.

Lastly, the opportunity—thanks to employees' and pensioners' contributions to the Canton of Vaud's state pension scheme—to finance a building that is destined to accommodate the élite of the future while they are studying was another aspect that fed the board's enthusiasm throughout the 29-month period from the groundbreaking to the moment when the President of the 2020 YOG's organizing committee was presented with the keys.

The completion of this unique structure on time and on budget, despite the many technical challenges involved, was made possible by the unwavering commitment of four key groups of collaborators.

First, the governing bodies and senior state officials of the Canton of Vaud, without whom the administrative and legal vicissitudes would have been insurmountable.

The engineers, architects, and site managers succeeded in interpreting the somewhat utopian design and building it efficiently.

The management representatives of the Canton of Vaud's state pensions fund, and Retraites Populaires, offered a valuable link between the client and the various stakeholders involved in the project's realization.

With their sound experience in the field, the two tenant organizations—the Fondation Maisons pour Étudiants Lausanne (Lausanne Student Housing Foundation) and the University of Lausanne—enabled the accommodation to be closely tailored to students' and academic guests' needs.

Despite the first few months of the building's occupation being marked by tough restrictions imposed in relation to the Covid-19 pandemic, the Vortex filled up immediately. The residents of the building clearly expressed their satisfaction with life in this 2.8-kilometer linear village.

Objective achieved! The following pages offer a fascinating testimony to the project's success.

Michel Berney, President of the Real Estate Investment Committee
of the Canton of Vaud's state pension fund (CPEV)

The circle is a metaphor for contrasting situations. A vicious circle leads from one disaster to another, and if you are going round in circles, it means the situation is hopeless. Happily there is also the virtuous circle, signifying ever-increasing success. The Vortex is unmistakably of the latter variety. It is satisfying to be able to point that out here, in the opening pages of a volume dedicated to an impressive piece of architecture.

I was able to follow the project from the initial sketches through to its use today by 1,100 university residents. The Vortex was born under a lucky star. It was spawned by dreams and necessity. We wanted the 2020 Youth Olympic Games to take place in the Canton of Vaud and the University campus at Lausanne needed new housing facilities. Thus, the building was an Olympic Village at the beginning of 2020, before it welcomed students and other academic guests later the same year.

The combination of sport and housing set off a process that allowed good ideas to be rigorously carried forward. The selected piece of land seemed unappealing at first but proved to suit the purpose well once it had been connected to the campus and the city. Above all, the Zurich-based architect Jean-Pierre Dürig had a stroke of genius when he imagined a circular village similar to China's historic Tulous, rising eight stories but with a single continuous ramp 2.8 kilometers long. Once the winner of the design competition had been chosen, and his proposal had been developed in close collaboration with the Canton of Vaud's Construction Department, the moment came for the government to hand the design drawings over to its pension fund (CPEV) and the Retraites Populaires pension company. Losinger Marazzi was then chosen to build the Vortex. I would like to pay tribute here to the remarkable range of skills that made it possible for this technically demanding building to be erected within 29 months without exceeding the tightly calculated budget of 156 million Swiss francs. Everyone worked to this ambitious goal and the project was a success.

The photographs illustrating this book show the magnificent result. The Vortex is one of those buildings—public or private—whose silhouette marks a site. Together with the Rolex Learning Center right nearby; soon the Unithèque holding 350,000 books, which is now under construction; the new International Olympic Committee headquarters at Vidy; the recently completed Museum of Fine Arts (MCBA); and the soon-to-be-completed Museums of Photography (Elysée), and Contemporary Design and Applied Art (mudac), it helps make the Canton of Vaud a spot that stands out on the global map of contemporary architecture. It is a source of pride; realization that stands to endure—a virtuous circle.

Pascal Broulis, Member of the Council of State in charge of public building programs for the Canton of Vaud

CIRCLES, CYLINDERS, AND SPIRALS

It is no accident that Leonardo da Vinci's "Vitruvian Man" ("The proportions of the human body according to Vitruvius," *c.* 1490, p. 50) is inscribed in a square and a circle, nor that the standing stones of Stonehenge (Wiltshire, UK, *c.* 2000 BC) are arranged in a ring. The circle, which has neither beginning nor end, is an ancient symbol of infinity. The dome of the sky and the visible horizon implied a round form that led early Egyptians, Mesopotamians, and Greeks to imagine the Earth as a flat disk floating in the oceans. The circular plan is also that of the oldest prehistoric dwellings. In early civilizations, circular forms appear frequently. In India and Indianized Asia, the sacred space of the mandala (p. 22) is a circle, considered by some to be magical. Hindu temples, seen in projection on a plane, form a mandala, and like the mandala they represent both a microcosm and a pantheon.

Examples of circular forms in art and architecture abound from the earliest times. The nimbus that haloed certain figures in antiquity originally expressed the radiation of the sun and other astral deities. The halo is round in accordance with the celestial symbolism of the circle. The zodiac, whose importance was so great for the ancients, the Romans, and in medieval times, still plays a role in the minds of some: for all of them, it is the wheel of life. In the Middle Ages the wheel of fortune illustrates many manuscripts, for example *Clavis physicae* by the Christian theologian Honorius of Autun in the 12th century, but is also seen on churches, where the rose window is sometimes a wheel of fortune. In the South Rose of Saint-Denis Cathedral (12th century) the central figure of God is surrounded by the 12 signs of the zodiac and 24 agricultural tasks.

Although it is said that a perfect circle is a "geometric idealization," there are many forms in nature that approach such perfection. These vary in size from microscopic plasmids, double-stranded DNA molecules that are distinct from a cell's chromosomal DNA, to so-called "ring galaxies," such as PGC 10000714, where a circle of younger stars surrounds an old galactic core, or Hoag's Object, a ring galaxy discovered in 1950 which has a radius of 60,500 light years (p. 45). Closer to our scale, a rainbow is an arc of a nearly perfect circle; a drop of rain generates circular ripples in a pond (p. 28); and orb weaver spider webs also adopt this universal form. Meteor-impact craters seen from above and the full moon (p. 39) itself also recall the omnipresence of circular shapes.

In the case of the Vortex building, which is the object of this book, there is also a central spiral ramp. Spirals are again signal forms in the natural world, from whirlpools and tornados to nautilus shells, or sunflowers (p. 18) with their convergent spiral seed patterns that are known to occur in numbers related to the Fibonacci sequence (0, 1, 1, 2, 3, 5, 8, 13, 21...), and on to great spiral galaxies, such as the Milky Way itself.

It is obvious that circles and spirals can be found throughout the natural world and, thus, they also figure in a prominent way in the architecture and art of every period and civilization. It should be noted that beyond natural forms, geometry has developed on the basis of volumes that might be called the intellectualized equivalent of the physical world. In geometry, too, the relation between essential forms has been studied since ancient times. The Greek mathematician, engineer, and astronomer Archimedes (*c.* 287–212 BC) derived an accurate approximation of the constant *pi* and went on to establish the relation between the surface area and volume of a sphere to a cylinder of the same height and diameter. A sphere and a cylinder are said to have marked the tomb of Archimedes in Syracuse, and so the "purest" geometric forms, intimately related to nature, are at the heart of mathematics and, so too, frequently present in architecture, for example. Circle, cylinder, and spiral can be considered "abstract" but they are also ingrained in nature and culture.

Spiral organization and circular form (tondo) are regularly present in art in the Renaissance and even before. Indeed, seeking different types of abstraction, modern artists have made powerful

It is obvious that circles and spirals can be found throughout the natural world and, thus, they also figure in a prominent way in the architecture and art of every period and civilization.

use of these shapes, which seem to have an instantaneous impact, surely because they are based on what might be called "primal" forms. Robert Smithson's 460-meter-long *Spiral Jetty* (Rozel Point, Great Salt Lake, Utah, 1970, p. 37) is one of these. Another is the *Target* series by the American artist Jasper Johns (p. 42), made essentially of concentric, colored circles. The idea of a "target," of course, gives this apparently abstract composition a reference in the "real" world, but the visual power of these works is undeniable.

Where architecture is concerned, the perceptual psychologist Rudolf Arnheim wrote: "A circle stresses its identity by the unbreakable coherence of its contour; it also establishes its center with compelling precision... An expanded field of forces... is confirmed by the concavity of the boundary façades..."[1] This reflection applies to the abstract circular or cylindrical form but, clearly, these forms are rooted in the realities of the universe as we know it. Examples of buildings that embrace the circle or the spiral abound. Suffice it here to refer to two iconic modern buildings, Frank Lloyd Wright's Solomon R. Guggenheim Museum (1959, p. 34) on Fifth Avenue in New York and the more recent Apple Park by Foster + Partners in Cupertino (California, 2017, p. 25). The most "iconic" element of this latter complex is the six-story Ring Building (two levels below ground), which has an outer circumference of 1,494 meters and provides working space for 12,000 people.

The architect of the Vortex building, Jean-Pierre Dürig, says clearly that he was not referencing natural or even built forms, instead seeking to resolve the equation of placing a large building for students on a relatively constrained site. Dürig says that he has "no objection" to other interpretations of the cylindrical/spiral form of the Vortex, but even the word "vortex" has connotations in the natural world: "A mass of fluid (such as a liquid) with a whirling or circular motion that tends to form a cavity or vacuum in the center of the circle and to draw toward this cavity or vacuum bodies subject to its action."[2]

In some sense it does not matter what the architect says he was trying to accomplish. It is a clear fact that his solution is intimately related to some of the most basic forms of nature, art, and architecture. The circle will always return because of its uncompromised continuity, its absolute perfection. The spiral will always be the pattern of growth and organization seen in myriad expressions from sunflowers to spinning galaxies. Circles, spirals, and cylinders are part of the basic vocabulary of forms in the natural world, but also the more abstract domain of geometry. The Vortex is a cylinder that contains a spiral around its inner circumference. The analogies to the most fundamental forms do not have to be reconfirmed; they are self-evident.

1 Rudolf Arnheim, *The Dynamics of Architectural Form*, University of California Press, Berkeley, 1977.
2 See https://www.merriam-webster.com/dictionary/vortex.

Taido Shufu (1776–1836), *Ensō*, ink on paper (detail). Traditionally drawn by Japanese Zen monks in a single gesture, the *ensō* symbolizes enlightenment, the universe, and *mu* (the void).

The rings in the trunks of almost all trees mark annual growth.
Rarely in a perfectly circular form, they tend, nonetheless, to be round.

Fujian Tulou, aerial view. A type of fortified, rammed-earth, rural dwelling created beginning in the 12th century in the mountainous areas of southeastern Fujian Province in China.

Robert Delaunay, *Premier disque* (First Disk), 1912–13, oil on canvas, 134.6 cm (diameter). The first abstract work by the French painter, influenced by Kandinsky's ideas about color.

Sunflower. Forming a circle from a series of spirals,
the pattern of seeds within a sunflower follows the Fibonacci sequence.

South Rose window of Notre-Dame Cathedral, Paris, France, *c.* 1255, 12.9 meters (diameter). The concentric circular pattern is centered on Christ triumphant reigning over Heaven, surrounded by his witnesses on earth.

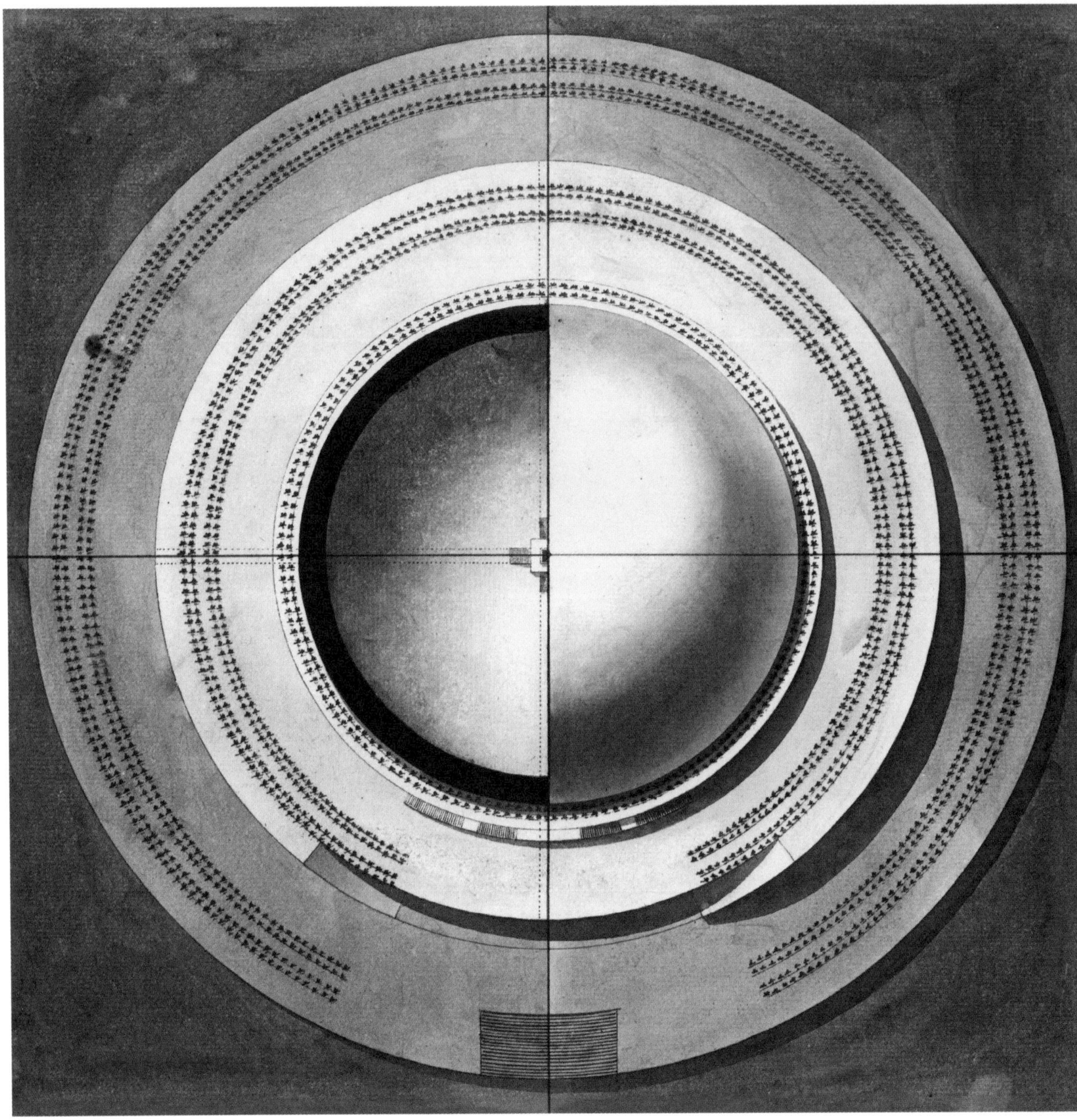

Étienne-Louis Boullée, *Plan of Newton's Cenotaph*, 1784.

A representation of Boullée's search for immutable forms in architecture.

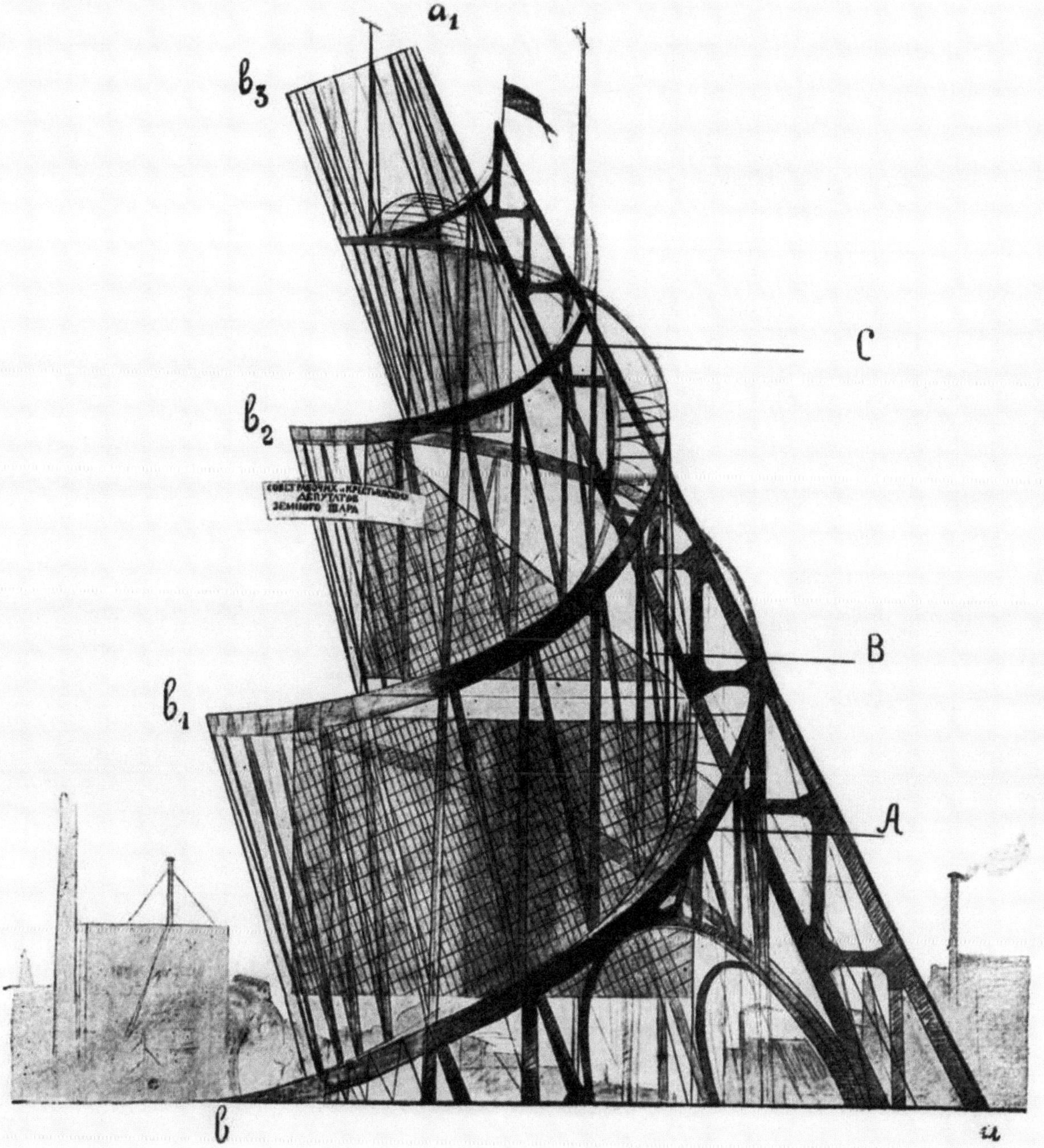

Vladimir Tatlin, *Monument to the Third International*, 1919.

Tatlin's leaning spiral tower was never built.

Thang Kha, Tibetan Buddhist mandala, 18th century. The mandala is a sacred diagram used for meditation and holy ceremonies.

Filippo Juvarra, Basilica of Superga, Turin, Italy, 1731. Interior view of the dome, which was completed in 1726.

Marcel Duchamp, *Rotorelief n°8-Cerceaux*, 1935. The *Rotoreliefs* are a series of decorated discs intended to spin on a turntable as optical entertainment.

Norman Foster, Apple Park, Cupertino, California, United States, 2017.

The Ring Building, seen here from above, has an outer circumference of 1,494 meters.

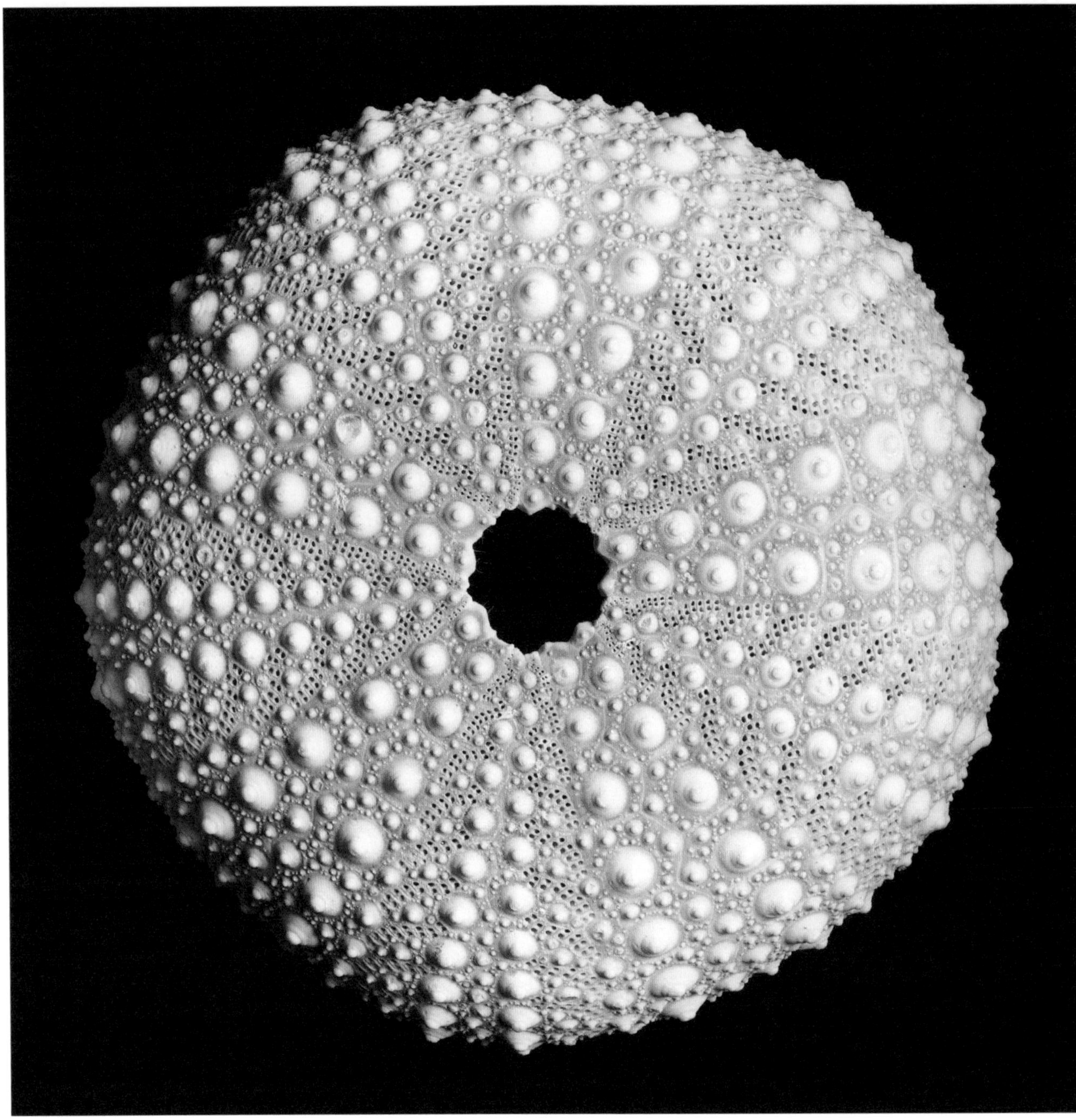

A dried sea urchin. Though apparently fragile, the calcium carbonate shells of sea urchins are inherently strong.

Jean Nouvel, Louvre Abu Dhabi, Abu Dhabi, United Arab Emirates, 2017.
An aerial view of the 180-meter, multilayered, lattice dome of the Museum.

Waterdrops. The concentric rings formed by drops of water when they fall vertically on a still body of water are among the most perfect circles in nature.

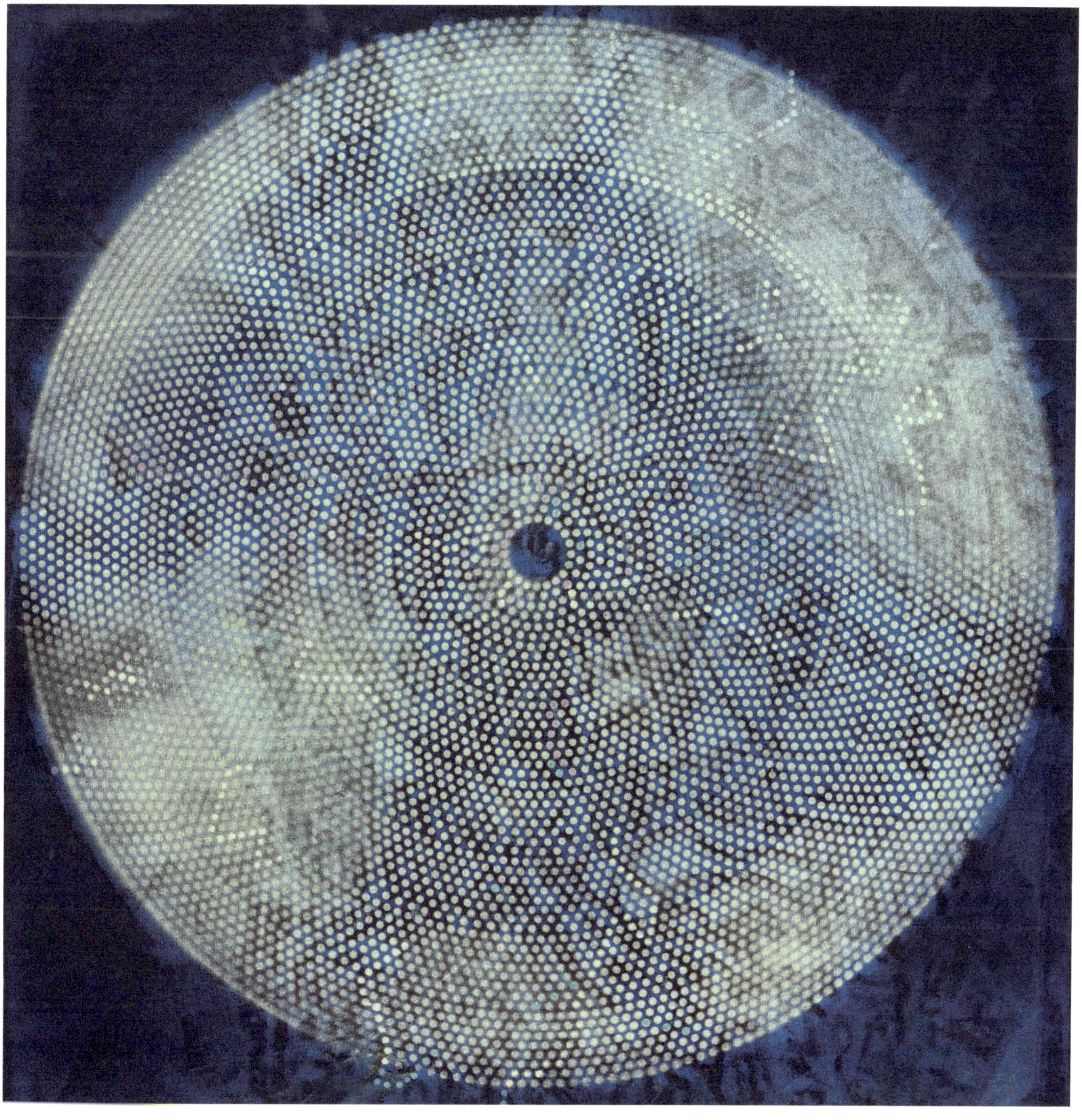

Max Ernst, *Birth of a Galaxy*, 1969, oil on canvas, 72 × 93 cm (detail).
Painted in the year of the first landing of men on the moon, this work "reflects upon man's yearning to explore other spheres..."

Marten van Valckenborch the Elder, *The Tower of Babel*, 1595, oil on panel, 105 × 75 cm. A spiraling ramp leading up the tower described in the Bible (Genesis 11:1–9).

Lundgaard & Tranberg, Tietgen Residence Hall, Copenhagen, Denmark, 2006.
A circular student residence with 360 rooms, but without a spiral connecting ramp like the one of the Vortex.

Round shield, Italian, wood covered with leather and parchment, diameter 50.5 cm, late 16th century. The round form is efficient, and has apparent connections to cosmology and nature.

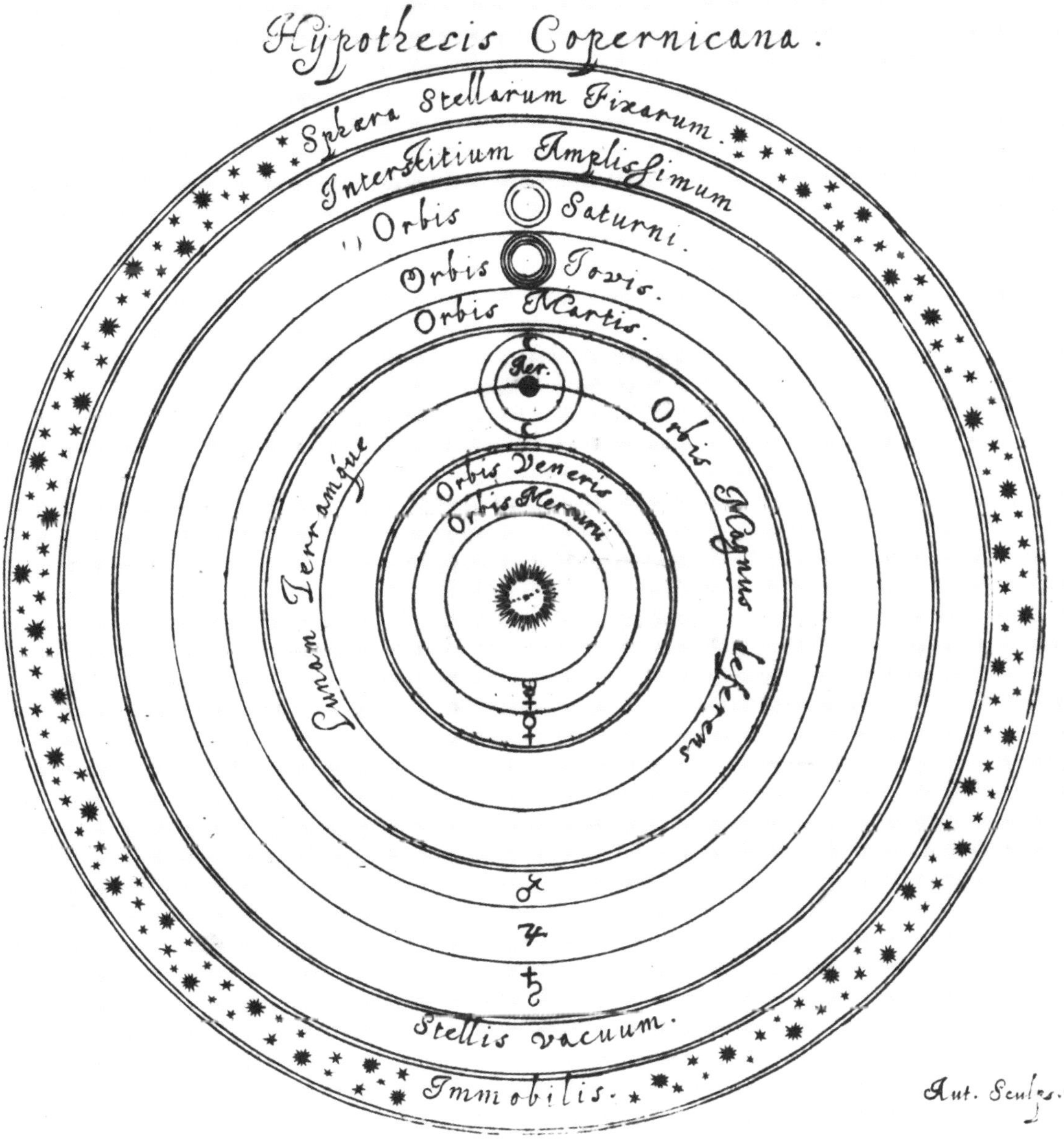

Johannes Hevelius, *Selenographia, sive Lunae descriptio* (Selenography, or a Description of the Moon), printed in 1647. A representation of the Cosmos of Copernicus.

Frank Lloyd Wright, Solomon R. Guggenheim Museum, New York, United States, 1959. Looking up toward the atrium dome, which is approached by a spiral ramp.

Victor Vasarely, Official Emblem for the Games of the XX Olympiad, Munich, Germany, 1972. A colorful, spiraling symbol for the Munich Olympics from the creator of Op Art.

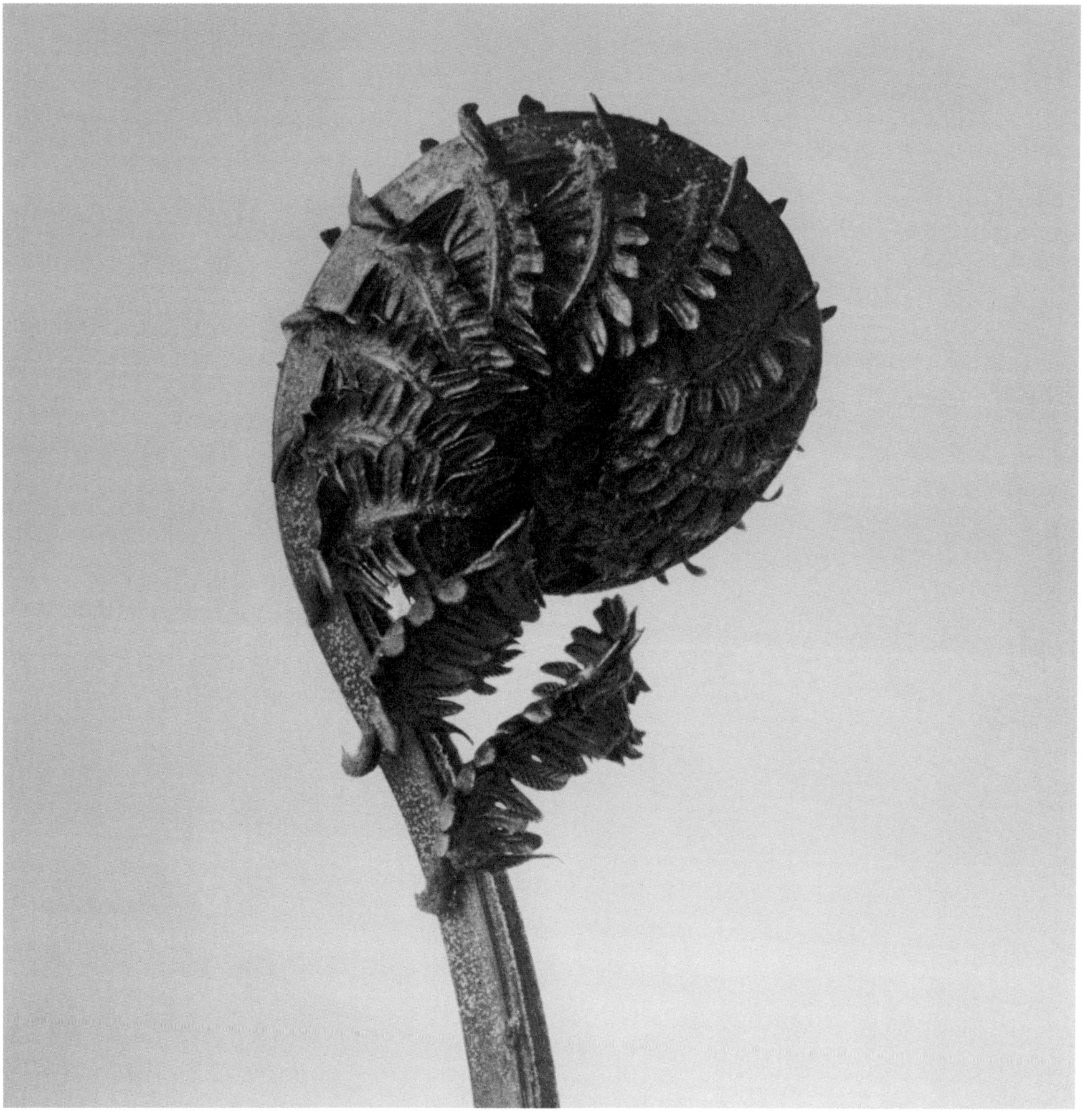

Karl Blossfeldt, *Matteuccia struthiopteris* (German Ostrich fern), 1928, photograph.

The endless cycle of growth and birth in a spiral form.

Robert Smithson, *Spiral Jetty*, Great Salt Lake, Utah, United States, 1970.
460 meters long and 4.6 meters wide, the work seeks to negate the viewer's sense of time and place.

Upper Jurassic serpenticone ammonite, 38 × 50 cm. An extinct marine mollusc whose name was inspired by the spiral shape of their fossilized shells.

A NASA photograph of the full moon, the most visible and obvious of the round (or spherical) forms in the night sky.

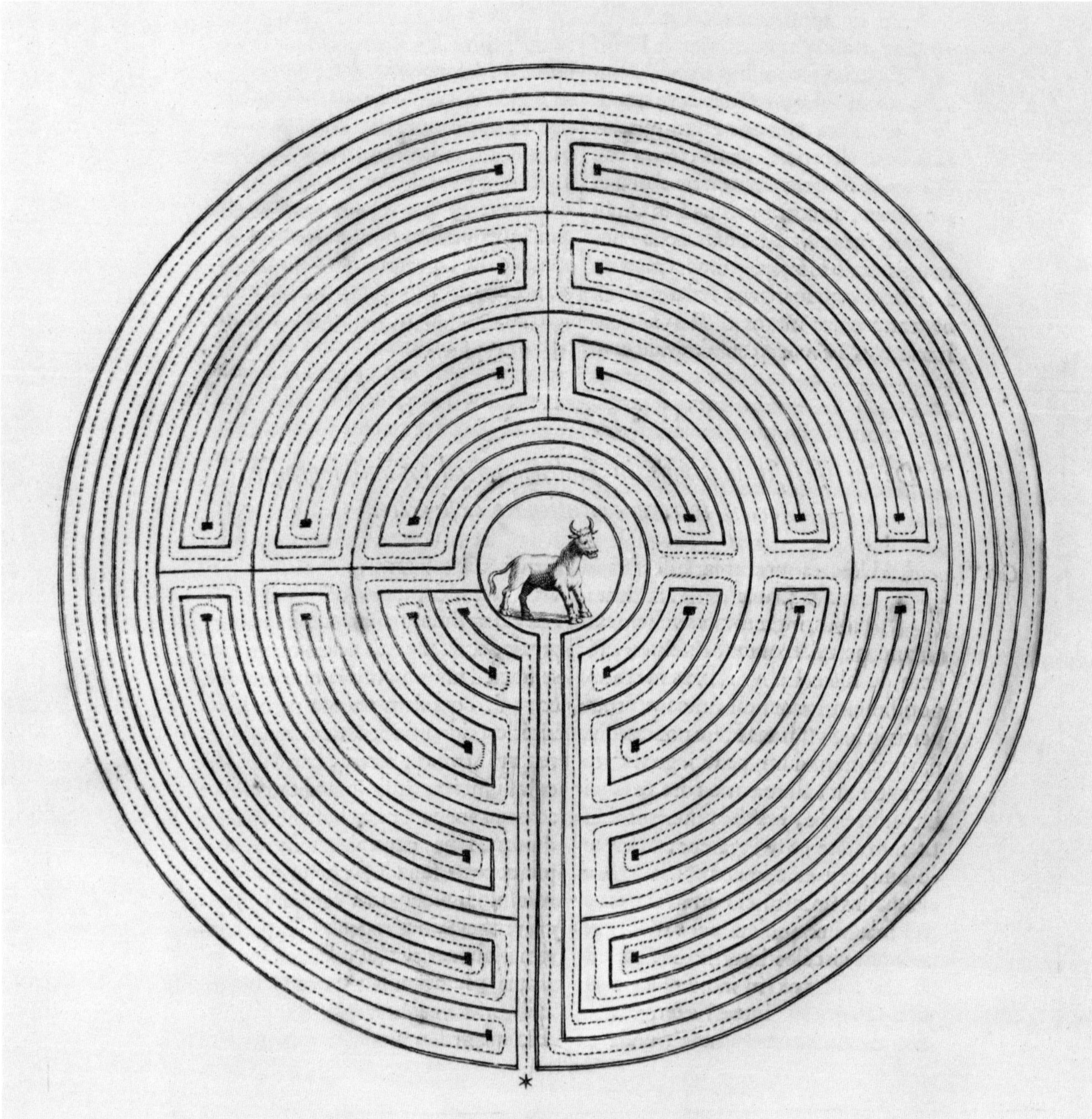

Athanasius Kircher, *Turris Babel*, published in 1679. An engraving representing the Minotaur's labyrinth as designed by Daedalus for King Minos of Crete.

Kengo Kuma, The Exchange in Darling Square, Sydney, Australia, 2019.
Twenty thousand meters of light-colored wood wrap around the building like a kind of "vortex."

Jasper Johns, *Target*, 1959, 37 × 36 cm.

One of a series of works on this theme, this painting combines a dart-board style target with a fundamental expression of color and form.

Hiroshi Nakamura, Ribbon Chapel, Onomichi, Japan, 2014.
Two intertwining spiral stairs symbolize marriage in this work, which is "composed only of paths."

Norman Foster, Reichstag, Berlin, Germany, 1999.
The architect added a glass dome and a double spiral of ramps
that looks down on the chamber of parliament.

Hoag's Object, a ring galaxy located 600 million light years from earth. The outer ring of blue stars is 120,000 light years wide, slightly larger than the Milky Way.

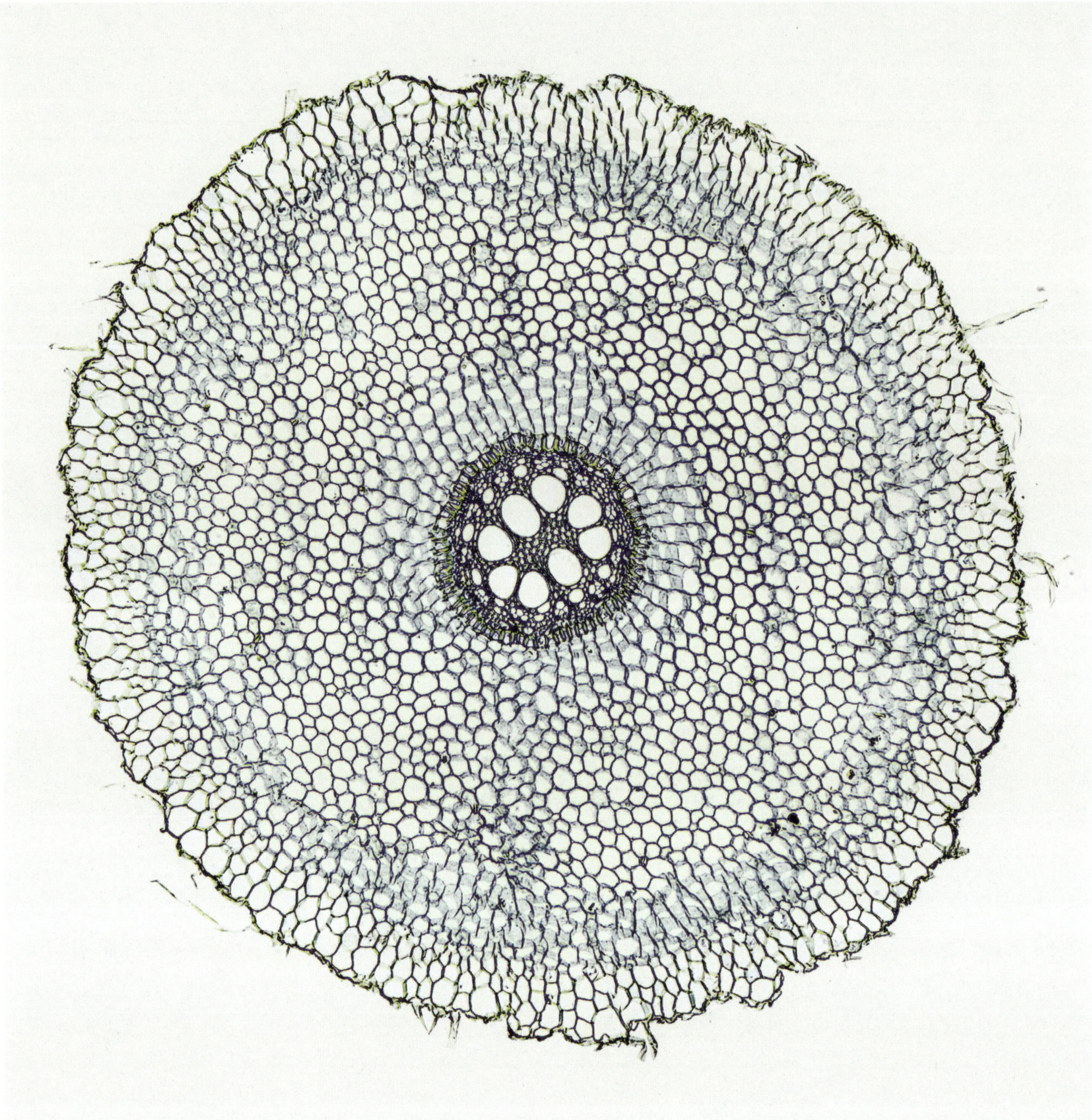

Iris pseudacorus, Yellow Iris, transverse section of a root. Though perfect circles are said to be a geometric abstraction, many natural forms approach fully round shapes.

Eugene Stamo (architect), Aleksandr Markelov (engineer), Bublik, Moscow, Russia, 1972. This round Soviet-era apartment building contains 913 apartments.

Devil's Bridge, Kromlau, Germany. Located in the Azalea and Rhododendron Park Kromlau, the Devil's Bridge, with its basalt columns, was designed to form a circle when reflected in the water.

Gjøde & Partnere, Infinite Bridge, Aarhus, Denmark, 2015. This circular structure is intended as a viewpoint over the Bay of Aarhus, the forest, and the Varna Palace.

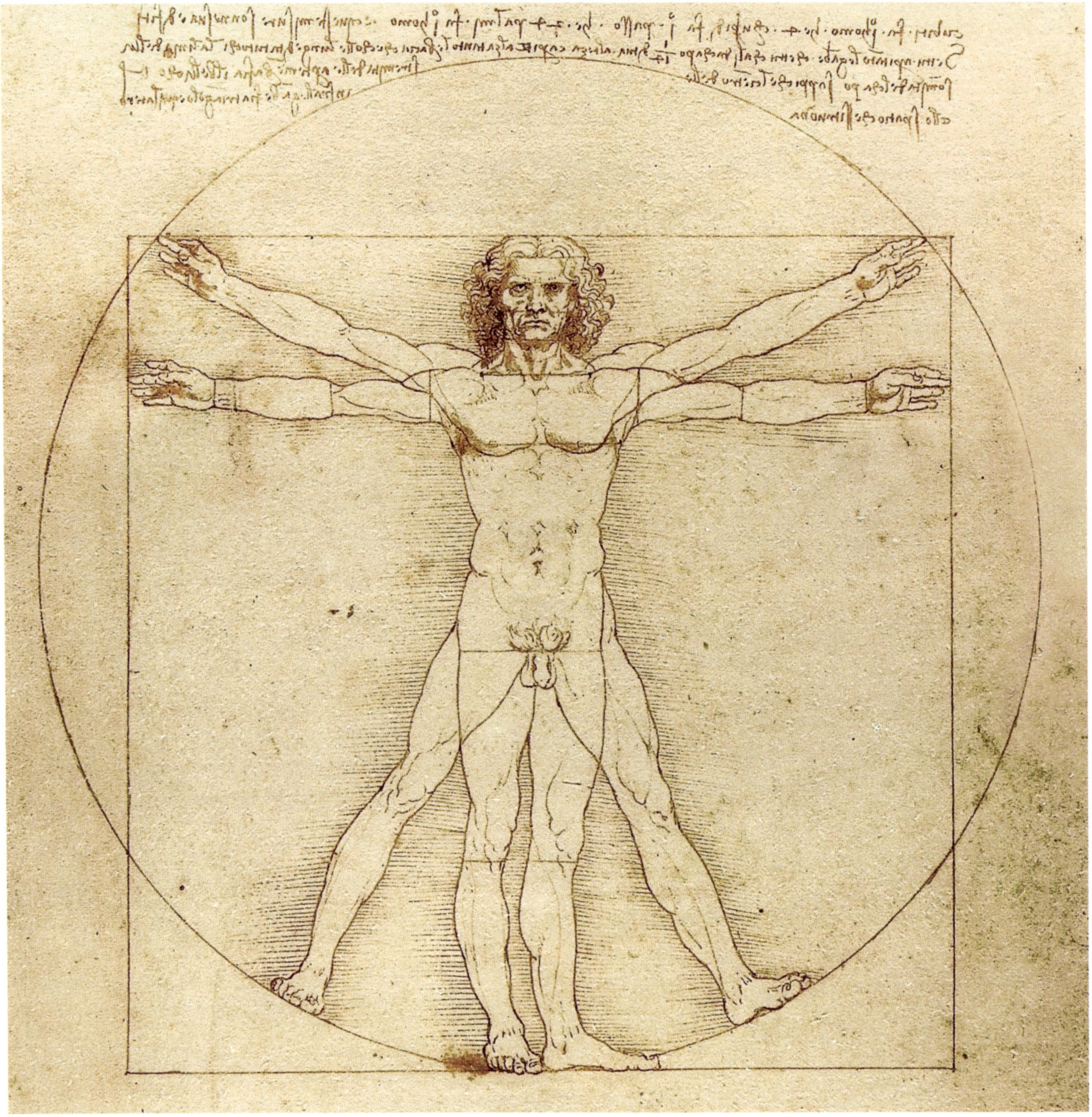

Leonardo da Vinci, "Vitruvian Man," *c.* 1490. This ink-on-paper drawing depicts the perfect proportions of man in two superimposed positions with arms and legs spread and inscribed in a circle and square.

Dürig AG + Itten+Brechbühl AG, Vortex, Chavannes-près-Renens, Switzerland, 2020.
Student housing for the University of Lausanne.

THE STORY OF THE VORTEX

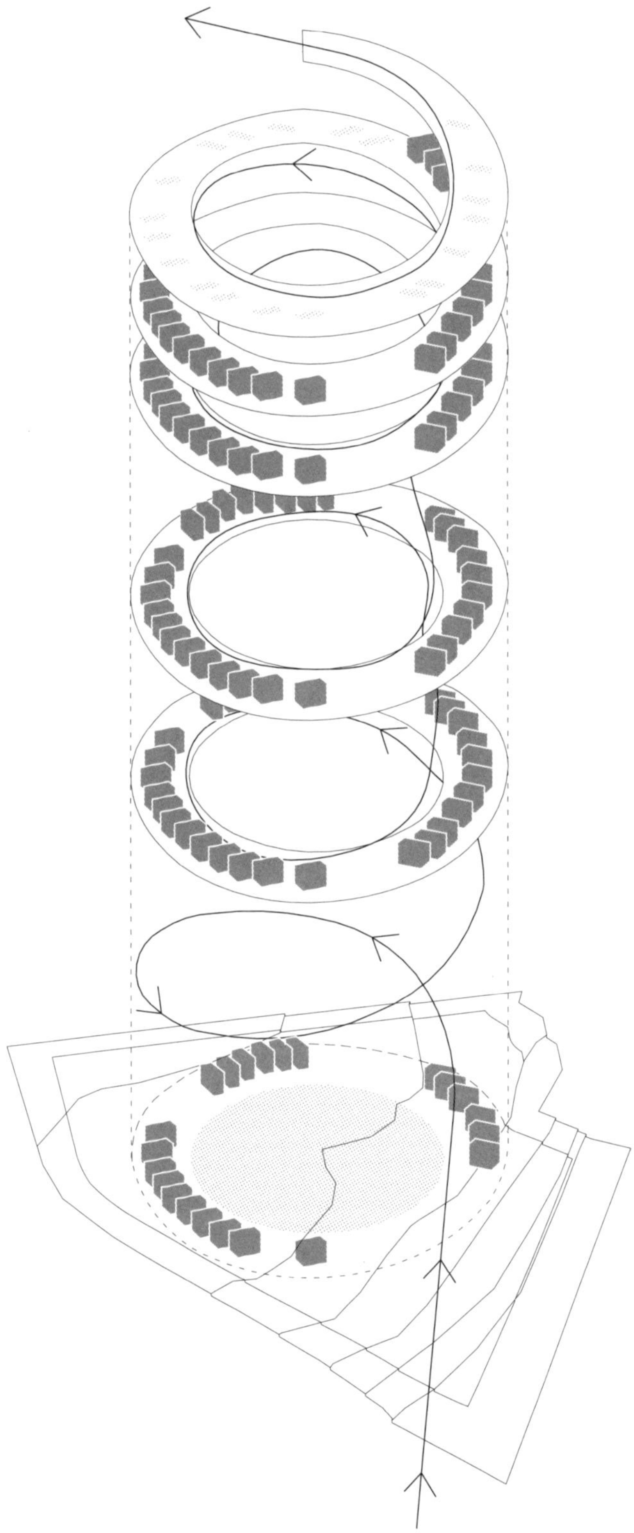

Concept drawing for the Vortex building by Jean-Pierre Dürig.

Imagined as a key element of Lausanne's bid for the 2020 Youth Olympic Games (YOG), the Vortex is an unusual student housing complex built on the site of the University of Lausanne at the behest of the authorities of the Canton of Vaud and carried forward by locally based pension funds. First imagined in 2014, the building was built between 2017 and 2019. It offers a floor area of 36,700 square meters and has a total of 941 bedrooms, as well as 2,400 square meters of shared spaces, including a restaurant and rooftop café, a daycare facility, a store, and flexible meeting spaces. The Vortex was first used to house 1,700 athletes who came to Lausanne for the YOG in January 2020. In use by the University of Lausanne, EPFL, and other schools since July 2020, it normally houses about 1,100 students, while also including some visiting professors or members of the University team. With an external diameter of 137 meters and an internal diameter of 105 meters, the 29-meter-high building is physically impressive. One of its most unusual features is a 2.8-kilometer-long ramp with a 1% inclination that forms a continuous path from ground level to the top of the building.

The realization of this complex project, which was carried out on schedule and on budget, can be attributed to the exceptional degree of communication and collaboration between entities and individuals that have varying degrees of official association with the Canton of Vaud. The architects and builders were, of course, not in this official category and the delicate balance necessary for a public-private partnership was also carried forward thanks to their knowledge and expertise. Some of the participants are presented here, and others comment in the next section of the book on the detailed process of program, competition, architectural design, and construction that gave a final result judged by all concerned to be very positive.

The texts that follow present reference points about the Dorigny campus where the UNIL/EPFL universities are located, the construction process and the organizations involved in the management of student housing, the Youth Olympic Games, and the owner of the building CPEV.

3 Emmanuel Borloz, "Les vraies raisons qui ont chassé l'Uni du centre-ville," *24Heures*, May 7, 2018. Available at: https://www.24heures.ch/vaud-regions/lausanne-region/vraies-raisons-chasse-uni-centreville/story/21986703 accessed January 8, 2021.

4 The facts cited here are from a Canton of Vaud document: https://www.vd.ch/fileadmin/user_upload/organisation/gc/fichiers_pdf/176_Texte_CE.pdf downloaded January 8, 2021.

A BRIEF HISTORY OF THE UNIVERSITY OF LAUSANNE

On September 4, 1963, the Canton of Vaud bought a 26-hectare plot situated to the west of Lausanne in the towns of Écublens, Saint-Sulpice, and Chavannes-près-Renens. Owned starting in the 17th century by the de Loys family, the so-called Dorigny site was the location of a large house built between 1770 and 1774, and various agricultural outbuildings. Occupied by the de Loys family until 1910, the house was rented to the Aga Khan from 1917 to 1950. Owned after 1938 by the Hoyos-de Loys family, the Dorigny property was the object of other development schemes because of its proximity to Lausanne, including a possible airport in 1946, before its purchase by the Canton and the decision in 1965 to dedicate the site to university development.[3]

The University of Lausanne (UNIL), today located on the Dorigny site, found its origins in the Academy, founded in 1537 as the first French-language Protestant school of theology. Located near the city's Cathedral, the so-called Ancienne Académie was built between 1579 and 1587. By the 18th century, the Academy began to teach science, law, and history. With the end of the domination of Bern in 1798, the Academy began to broaden its horizons with professorships in theology, literature, science, law, and medicine. In 1890, the Academy formally became the University of Lausanne, and 16 years thereafter moved to a new home. Located on the eastern side of Place de la Riponne at the base of the hill where the city's Cathedral (1275) and the former Académie are located, the Palais de Rumine was built between 1891 and 1906 as planned by the architect Gaspard André. The building was designed to house the University, the library of the Canton, and several art and science museums. The Florentine Renaissance style of the building is without any clear relation to local tradition, but was thought appropriate in terms of references to a time of cultural renewal and humanism.

By the 1960s, the desire of the Canton to develop the University began to imply a move out of the overcrowded facilities in the city. The purchase of the Dorigny property was the first major step toward creating a veritable new campus, as the Canton purchased several other neighboring lots bringing the available plot up to 35.4 hectares in 1965, adding a further 8.8 hectares in 1968. By 1970, the campus had a total area of 74.5 hectares.[4] A committee was established in 1966 to plan the future campus, which would include not only the University of Lausanne, but also the former École Polytechnique de l'Université de Lausanne (EPUL), which became the École Polytechnique Fédérale de Lausanne (EPFL) in 1968. The transfer of the UNIL and EPFL to the Dorigny campus began in 1970. The first building of the UNIL, the Amphipôle, was built in 1969–70 by Guido Cocchi (1928–2010), who was the chief architect of the UNIL between 1971 and 1995. The inauguration of the first EPFL buildings on the new campus took place in 1978. The UNIL had 15,868 students for the Fall 2019 semester, while the EPFL had 11,449. The Dorigny site presently covers 90 hectares and has 35 buildings, with five further structures planned in the next eight years.

← Johann-Jakob Biedermann and Gabriel-Ludwig Lory (engraver). View of the area of Lausanne, 1783–1830, print.

→ Aerial view of the Dorigny site and the plain of Ecublens, 1953.

→→ Aerial view of the Dorigny site with the Vortex in construction upper right, 2019.

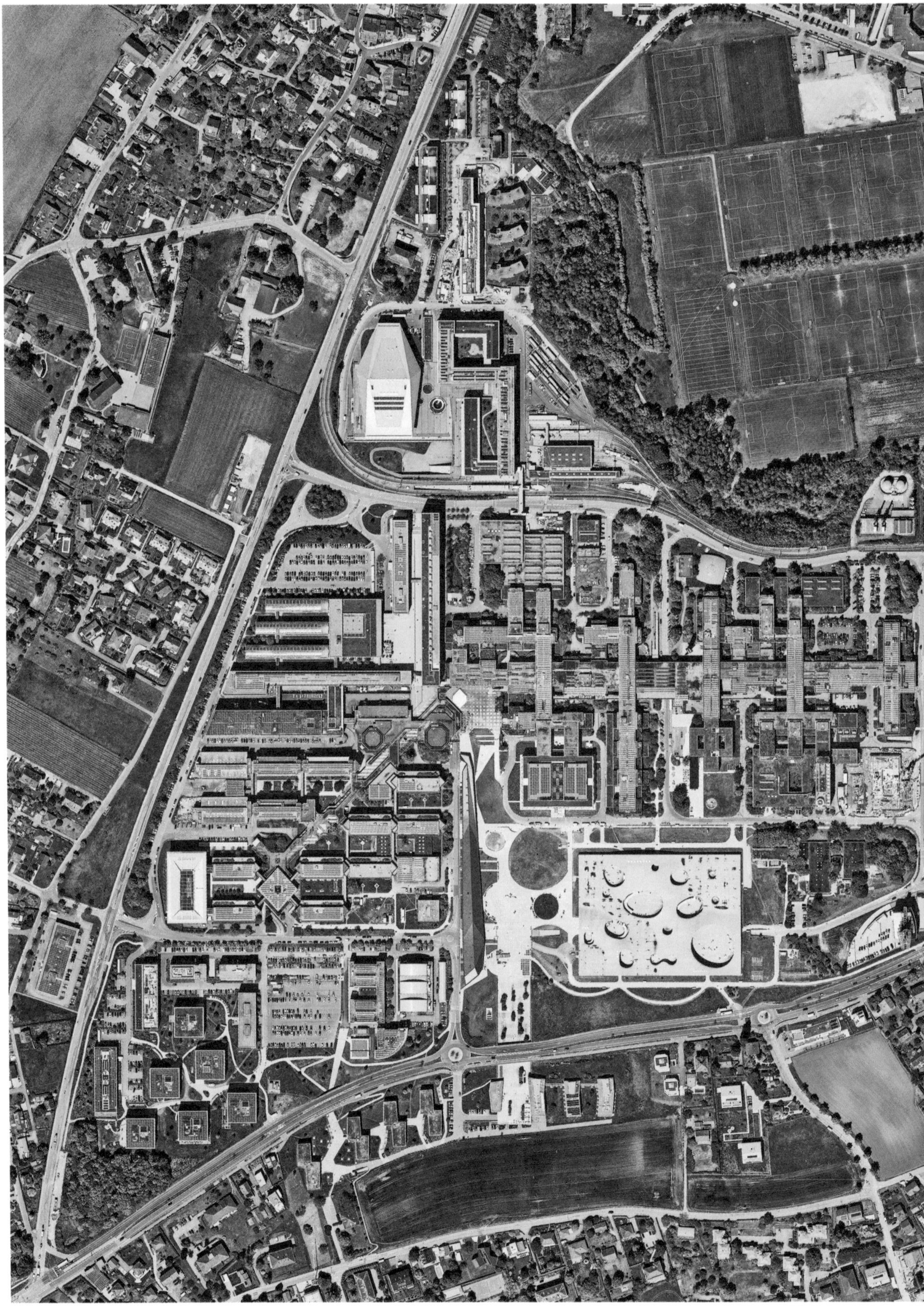

Losinger & Cie was a civil engineering and construction company founded in 1917 in Burgdorf, Switzerland, by the brothers Oskar and Eugen Losinger. By the 1960s it was the largest international Swiss construction firm. In 1990 the Losinger family ceded control of the firm to the French builder Bouygues. In 2006, Losinger Construction took over the Marazzi Group, which had been founded in 1907 in Bern. Losinger Marazzi currently employs 800 people in Switzerland and has an annual turnover of about 800 million Swiss francs. The firm has worked recently on such projects as the Rolex Learning Center (Kazuyo Sejima + Ryue Nishizawa / SANAA, EPFL, Lausanne, 2010), the Prime Tower (Gigon/Guyer, Zurich, 2011), and the Jan Michalski Foundation (Vincent Mangeat and Pierre Wahlen, Montricher, 2014). As the result of a competition, Losinger Marazzi was selected as the general contractor for the Vortex project, in association with the Lausanne office of the architects Itten+Brechbühl on February 16, 2017. They were the only firm to affirm their capacity to build the project as it was designed, and to deliver it on time and on budget, a task that they accomplished very precisely.

The head of the project for Losinger Marazzi was Eric Burg, a French native who had previously worked on the Rolex Learning Center for the firm. His description of the involvement of Losinger Marazzi is a clear indication of the exemplary nature of the firm's commitment and expertise.

Philip Jodidio
How were you involved in the Vortex?

Eric Burg
I started working on this project in December 2016, and I was in charge of the construction for Losinger Marazzi. I never met Jean-Pierre Dürig, but I did, of course, work closely with Itten+Brechbühl in Lausanne. Together, we did everything possible to conserve the image of the project while still reducing costs in the required proportions.

PJ
What were some of the challenges that the construction implied?

EB
The spiral structure was technically difficult to realize, and we were tasked with finding ways to build the design in an optimal way. We looked around the world and of course found circular buildings or spiral designs, but nothing with this form and on this scale. Two structures we identified were the Bublik, a circular apartment building in Moscow (Eugene Stamo, architect, and Aleksandr Markelov, engineer, 1972, p. 47) which has parallel horizontal circular floors, and, of course, the Guggenheim in New York (Frank Lloyd Wright, 1959, p. 34), which has a more inclined spiral ramp. The idea was that when you walk around the full diameter, you go up one floor. One difficulty was that the necessary reasoning for the architects and the engineers had to correspond to each other and to the actual construction process, which poses different issues when the plans are being prepared. There are many apparently small issues involved, such as the fact that because of the inclination of the ramps, there are slight variations in the height of the apartment door sills—they vary between a flat surface and a nine-centimeter added height. It is a bit like what is done in mountain villages where there are often triangular door sills corresponding to the degree of inclination of the road. There are, of course, handrails along the entire 2.8-kilometer length of the spiral ramp. In a somewhat unusual procedure, these were put in place as we did the concrete formwork for the ramp. This permitted us to avoid scaffolding and the costs of temporary handrails during construction.[5]

5 Eric Burg in conversation with the author, Lausanne, September 20, 2020.

"The spiral structure was technically difficult to realize, and we were tasked with finding ways to build the design in an optimal way." EB

9H
10H
11H

12H
1H

ramelet
fils

READY FOR THE YOUTH OLYMPIC GAMES

The Youth Olympic Games, for 14- to 18-year-old athletes, have been held every two years since 2010, when the event was organized in Singapore. Like the version for adults, they alternate every two years between Summer and Winter Games. The 2020 Lausanne Youth Olympic Games were held from January 9–20, 2020. A total of 1,872 athletes from 79 countries participated in the events, which were organized mostly in the Canton of Vaud, centered on Lausanne. Lausanne's credentials to host the Games are well known. It is where the headquarters of the International Olympic Committee (IOC) are located in the newly built Olympic House (3XN, Itten+Brechbühl, 2019). To celebrate its 100th anniversary in 1994, the IOC officially designated Lausanne as the Olympic Capital, and one year later the city inaugurated its Olympic Museum on the shores of Lake Geneva (Léman). Approximately 50 international sports organizations and federations also have their headquarters in Lausanne.

A press communiqué of the Canton announced the candidacy of Lausanne on June 26, 2013. On November 28 of the same year, it was announced that two cities were in competition—Lausanne and Brașov in Romania. Lausanne was selected on July 28, 2015, at the 128th IOC Session in Kuala Lumpur. A temporary skating rink for short track speed skating and figure skating events was built at Malley but the Vortex project, originally imagined as the Olympic Village, was a centerpiece of the candidacy of Lausanne. Indeed, one strength of Lausanne and the other areas involved in the Games was that a limited amount of new construction was required. Although the architect did not speak in such terms, the Vortex was immediately imagined as being one of the Olympic rings. It is true that both the number of rooms in the building and its opening date were closely related to the Games. A total of about 1,700 people were lodged there during the Games, two per room. As scheduled, the keys to the complex were given to the organizers of the Games on October 31, 2019, and athletes stayed there during the events. In fact, the 2020 event marked the first time that all of the participating delegations in any edition of the Olympics stayed in one building. The so-called Yodli Café[6] was installed in a tent in the circular courtyard of the building, encouraging precisely the kind of social interaction that seduced the competition jury when they selected Jean-Pierre Dürig's project. Thereafter, more precisely as of July 2020, the use of the building was placed in the hands of the FMEL and the UNIL.

The 2020 event won the "Best Winter Sports Competition 2019/2020" at the Winter Sports TOPS Awards in Beijing.

6 Yodli, mascot of the Lausanne 2020 YOG.

A total of 1,700 athletes were lodged in the Vortex during the Lausanne 2020 Youth Olympic Games in January 2020.

Flags of countries participating in the Youth Olympic Games
on the façade of the Vortex, January 2020.

SUI
SUI
SUI

JAPAN
JAPAN
JAPAN

7 Chantal Ostorero in conversation with the author, Lausanne, October 5, 2020.

A FOUNDATION FOR STUDENT HOUSING

The FMEL (Fondation Maisons pour Étudiants Lausanne) is a Swiss non-profit organization that provides housing to students attending the University of Lausanne (UNIL), the Swiss Federal Institute of Technology of Lausanne (EPFL), the Canton of Vaud's higher education institutions (HES), and the Higher School of Pedagogy of Lausanne (HEP). The FMEL was founded in 1961 by the City of Lausanne, the Canton of Vaud, and the University of Lausanne. At present it houses approximately 2,500 students in 14 different locations, mostly in the area of Lausanne. The FMEL is governed by a Board of Trustees composed of representatives of the Canton of Vaud, the City of Lausanne, the University of Lausanne, and the Swiss Federal Institute of Technology of Lausanne, as well as three students from the UNIL, EPFL, or a higher education institution. The FMEL has been in charge of renting 829 student accommodations in the Vortex building since July 2020. The UNIL itself rents rooms in the building for visiting professors and other persons associated with the University. According to Chantal Ostorero, President of the FMEL, the timing of the Vortex project deserves to be considered in the context of other events. In 2010–12 there was a housing crisis for students in the area. Some even had to go to a camping ground as the FMEL searched for apartments. Chantal Ostorero, who participated in each phase of the Vortex project, explains:

"My predecessor had, in fact, tried to develop a housing project of about 400 rooms for the site at La Pala in 2010, but one problem at that time was its relative exiguity. I heard in 2014 that the Canton was a candidate for the 2020 Youth Olympic Games and that housing was needed for the athletes. It was obvious in this instance that there was a good reason to create permanent lodging that could serve the universities after the Youth Olympic Games were over. We worked on the program for the new building with the Canton and the UNIL because the FMEL is functionally well aware of the housing needs of students. It was important for all concerned to create a lively, active place and not a sort of 'ghetto.' This brought the idea of a daycare center, a store, and sports facilities. We realized that some savings were required and parts of the program had to be set aside after the competition, but what was essential remained. The political authorities worked out the financing by agreeing with the CPEV that they would be the owners. I was a member of the jury for the project. I found the Dürig project intriguing from the beginning—it was at once very large and yet convivial. We knew that the spiral would be difficult to build, but it was fascinating as a concept. We also knew that costs had to be controlled so that students could afford to rent apartments. As far as the FMEL was concerned, we wanted to participate in the creation of a building of architectural interest, something that would take its place in local architectural heritage, much as the Rolex Learning Center at the EPFL (Kazuyo Sejima + Ryue Nishizawa / SANAA, 2010) has affirmed itself. I was personally in favor of the Vortex project. The ramp links all the residents and the round building uses the available site to its greatest advantage."[7]

> "It was obvious that there was a good reason to create permanent lodging that could serve the universities after the Youth Olympic Games were over." CO

CLOSE COLLABORATION: THE OWNER OF THE VORTEX

The Caisse de pensions de l'Etat de Vaud (CPEV, Pension Fund of the State of Vaud) was created in 1952 essentially for civil servants. The Retraites Populaires (RP), based in Lausanne, provides company and private pensions. Created as a public-law institution by the government of Vaud in 1902, the Retraites Populaires is responsible for the management of the CPEV. With approximately 200,000 clients, the Retraites Populaires had 27 billion Swiss francs in assets under management at the end of 2019. As part of its investment activity, it is the largest real-estate owner in French-speaking Switzerland, administering 14,000 accommodations located in 564 buildings. Its statutes remain those of a non-profit public-law institution. Its purpose is to facilitate access to its pension products and services for the entire population and to control its long-term commitments. In particular, it manages the real-estate assets owned by the CPEV, the Caisse intercommunale de pensions (CIP), and its own properties.

In the case of the Vortex project, which was initiated by the Canton of Vaud and built on land originally belonging to the government within the perimeter of the University of Lausanne, it was decided to cede the land to the pension funds so that they would finance and carry forward the construction. Beginning in 2016, the CPEV financed and carried out the project, whose cost was 156 million Swiss francs, with the Retraites Populaires acting as project manager. A further six million Swiss francs were added to the budget by the Canton for the public aspects of the installation. In compliance with the CPEV's real-estate investment policy, the Vortex project provides returns that are used to pay the pensions and benefits of those insured. It has also permitted the CPEV to diversify its investments and to participate directly in the local economy. Acting on the basis of long-term contracts, the UNIL and FMEL rent the building from the CPEV, which remains the owner. In turn UNIL and FMEL are responsible for renting the apartments to students and some people associated with the University.

On the occasion of the remittal of the keys to the Vortex to the organizing committee of the Lausanne 2020 Youth Olympic Games on October 31, the Board of Directors of the CPEV thanked the future users of the building—the Fondation Maison pour Étudiants Lausanne (FMEL) and the University of Lausanne (UNIL)—and, in particular, the Retraites Populaires, "which conducted the project efficiently and professionally," with the support of the services of the Canton of Vaud. It is a fact that the different organizations involved collaborated in a very efficient way, enabling the project to be completed on time and on budget. This is officially a public-private project, but this level of successful interaction is, of course, in part related to the different organizations involved, all of which have close ties to the government of the Canton of Vaud.

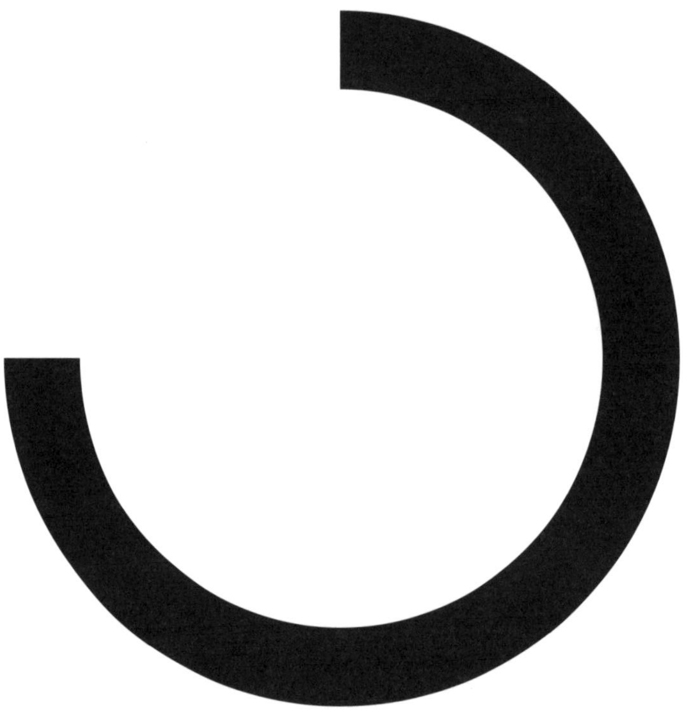

PORTFOLIO

60

7H

l'Amphimax

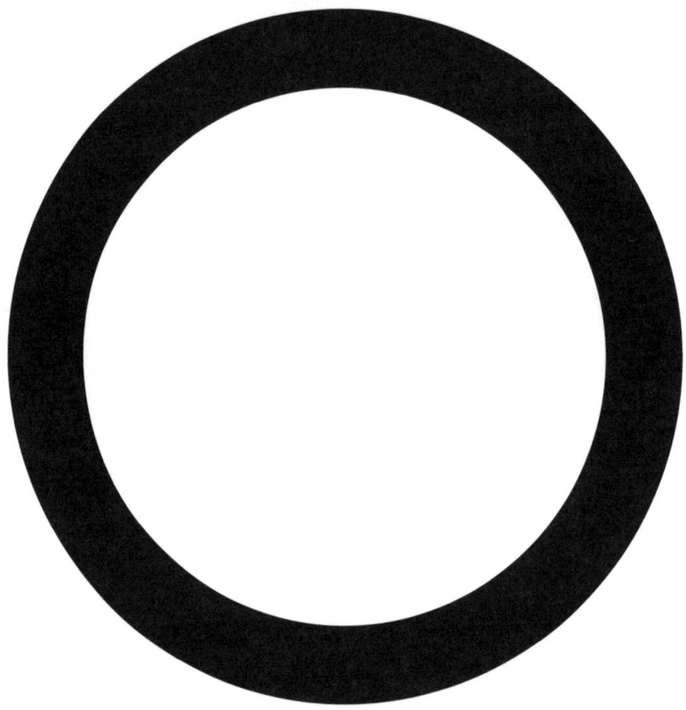

THE BUILDING AND ITS ARCHITECT

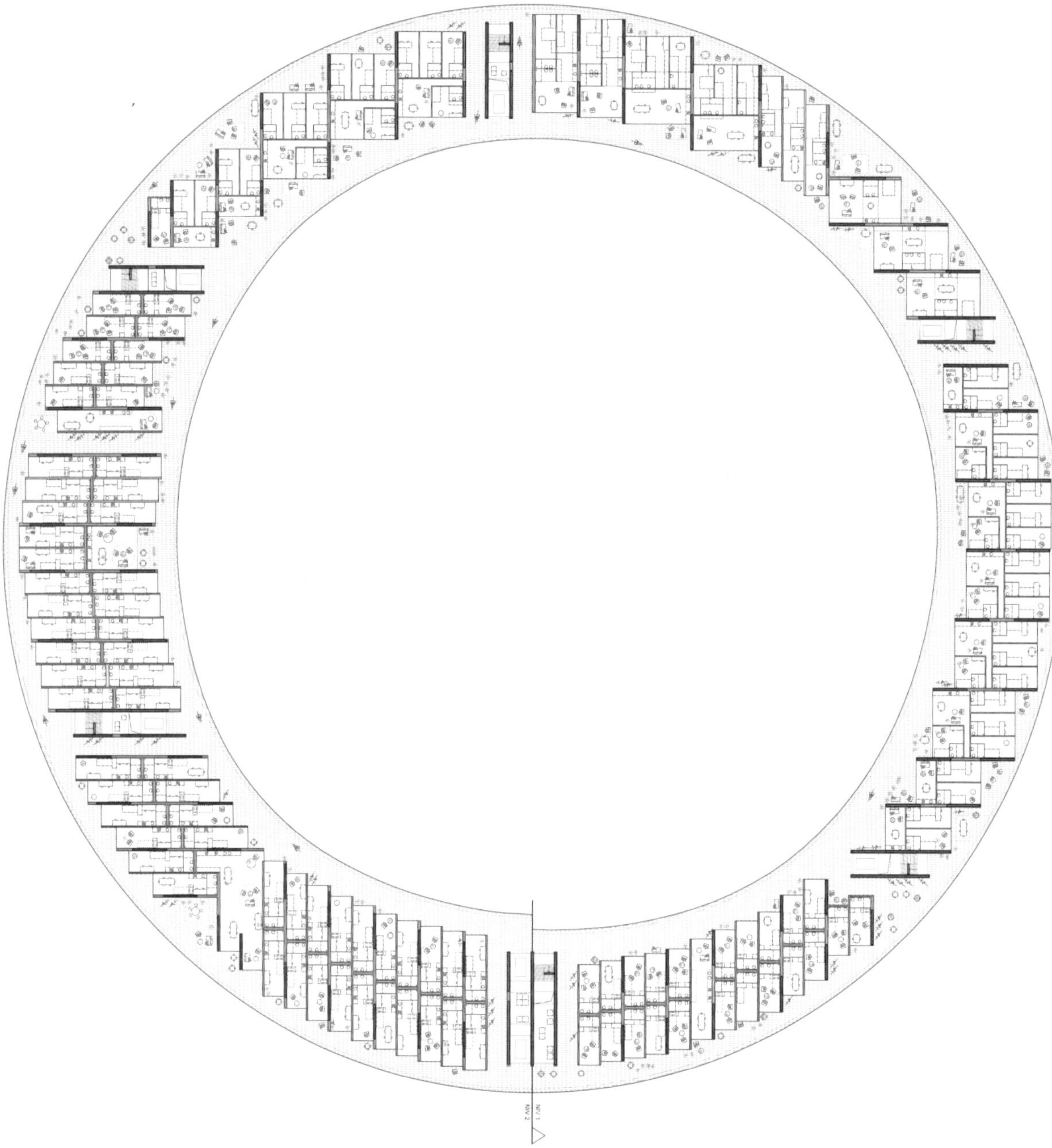

Plan of the first and second levels by Jean-Pierre Dürig, first phase of the competition.

From the initial expertise that found the Vortex entry to the competition for student housing on the grounds of the University of Lausanne (UNIL) to be problematic, to its completion, the Vortex posed challenges in relation to its unexpected design. This was particularly the case of the ramp, which runs along the internal circumference of the circular building. With its 1% inclination, construction was sure to be a difficult task given the nature of the building and its rapid schedule. Related to the forms of nature and rooted in history and culture, even as its architect sought to underline a purely functional solution to an architectural problem, the Vortex has already affirmed itself as an iconic presence in the region and in Switzerland.

UTOPIAN REALITY: GENESIS AND CONSTRUCTION OF THE VORTEX

Major architectural projects, and perhaps in particular those that rely on a public-private partnership, are by nature complex. Substantial disagreements are more the rule than they are the exception. The Vortex project can be cited as an exception to this rule, surely because of the structure and origins of the participating organizations, but also because of the professional qualities and positive will of the main participants. The idea for the Vortex came from a political decision to promote the candidacy of Lausanne and the Canton of Vaud for the 2020 Youth Olympic Games. Created in 2010, these Games are a substantial event, even if they are not on the scale of the adult Summer and Winter Olympic Games. Building on the very close connections between the Swiss city and the International Olympic Committee (IOC), and taking advantage of existing infrastructure in the region, the candidacy of Lausanne was crafted to provide one facility that could fill a substantial gap in the city's resources. Despite having a large student population located on the so-called Dorigny campus just outside the city, in the University of Lausanne (UNIL) and the Swiss Federal Institute of Technology of Lausanne (EPFL), the area had a well-known short fall in student housing. The Dorigny campus was designed to be "empty at night," as the Vice-Rector of the University puts it. Unlike most American universities that include student dormitories and apartments, the UNIL/EPFL complex had just one 550-room facility on campus for over 30,000 students.

Taking advantage of land that was available for construction on the campus, the Canton of Vaud, which owns the site, decided to build a residence for the 1,700 athletes anticipated for the 2020 Youth Olympic Games. This building would then be turned over for use by the University on a long-term basis. This efficient idea was a ready solution to the problem of infrastructure that has often gone unused after earlier Olympic events. As it was possible to lodge two athletes in each apartment, as opposed to single occupancy in the University, a basic size of 850 rooms was the starting point of the architectural competition organized beginning at the end of October 2014. The entire project was on a rapid schedule, since the building had to be ready for the athletes in January 2020. Making the entire project possible in terms of financing was accomplished by selling the selected site to the CPEV, the retirement fund of employees of the Vaud government. As the largest real-estate owner in the Canton (with its associated public retirement organization, the Retraites Populaires), this organization has substential experience in residential properties.

The competition, launched by the Canton and its own property and development arm the SIPaL, was organized by the DAI (Direction de l'Architecture et de l'Ingénierie). The jury President was the chief Architect of the Canton, Emmanuel Ventura. Other participants included Benoît Frund, Vice-Rector of the UNIL, Chantal Ostorero, President of the FMEL, which is the foundation tasked with managing student housing in the Lausanne area, and Philippe Pont, Director General of the SIPaL. Although technically a public-private partnership, the housing scheme relied on organizations—such as the CPEV, the UNIL and the FMEL—that are closely associated with the Canton. All concerned were positively engaged and their level of professional expertise was undeniable—these factors all contributed to an exceptional competition followed by a very efficient construction process. The general contractor selected, Losinger Marazzi, is a Swiss-based affiliate of the French construction giant Bouygues, with experience on the Dorigny campus since they built the Rolex Learning Center (Kazuyo Sejima + Ryue Nishizawa / SANAA, 2010). The people most closely involved in the Vortex project have been willing to explain their participation, their thoughts, and opinions. Taken together, the interviews published here represent a good

The idea for the Vortex came from a political decision to promote the candidacy of Lausanne and the Canton of Vaud for the 2020 Youth Olympic Games.

record of the inner workings of the jury and the construction process, as well, of course, as the original architectural concept and its evolution into a completed building. There is some intentional overlapping in the questions and responses, of interest because of the slightly different take of each participant, but also because some of the major aspects of the project are underlined—this is in particular the case of the idea of living together that inspired the jury and animated the design and construction process. One particularity of the overall project is that the competition-winning architect, Jean-Pierre Dürig, did not participate in the final construction process. The reasons for this are explained here, and the ability of the project managers to overcome this change is also an indication of the professionalism of those concerned. In any case, everything possible was done to maintain the spirit and concept of the original design.

Presiding the Jury

Since the housing project was launched at the level of the government of the Canton, the office for construction and new projects, entitled the SIPaL, was in charge of the development of the program and the architectural competition. The Cantonal Architect, Emmanuel Ventura, was thus a key participant from the outset. Here, he explains his point of view about the competition and the subsequent construction. With his position of Cantonal Architect, Ventura has an overarching view that includes both the design aspects of the project and also its urban impact.

Philip Jodidio
As President of the jury for the competition, how did you engage with this process?

Emmanuel Ventura
This was one of the first competitions I presided over as Architect of the Canton of Vaud. For this competition we had a kind of grid of questions or criteria made up to assist the jury with the advice of a broad variety of specialists in architecture and construction. These specialists were an architect, an urban designer, a landscape architect, and a sociologist; and there was a civil engineer, an engineer specialized in ventilation and heating. They were meant to give green, orange, red, and black ratings in terms of feasibility. Black meant that the specialists considered that it was not possible to select a given project. For the Vortex project by Jean-Pierre Dürig, these ratings were black along the whole line. Even the sociologist said that living together in such a large building would be difficult. According to our own rules, the black marks given to the Vortex should have meant that it would be eliminated from the competition even before being considered by the jury. Nonetheless, I spoke to members of the jury and, at my suggestion, they accepted to include the Vortex project in the competition because of its formal and architectural interest.

PJ
How did you come to the conclusion that the Vortex was the best project of the competition?

EV
Projects were eliminated by the jury and by the time we reached the final seven, the Vortex was still retained. After four hours of deliberation, however, there was still no clear choice among the finalists. The jury members all made it clear that they favored the Vortex, but did not really dare to vote for it because of the negative opinions of the specialists. I took it on myself to say that there was only one project that represented the future, and a kind of utopia. I said that in spite of the reservations of the experts, we could build this project on time and on budget. The jury then selected the Vortex by a unanimous vote.

PJ
Despite your strong engagement in favor of the Vortex, you had something of a surprise when you informed the architect, Jean-Pierre Dürig, of his victory, did you not?

Computer-generated images of the Vortex provided by Jean-Pierre Dürig.

EV

Absolutely. When I first announced to him on the phone that he had been selected for this student housing project, he understood that he had won a Special Mention and not the overall competition. He imagined that his design would exist on paper only. He has entered over a thousand competitions and it seems clear that his competitive drive may be stronger than his real will to build.

PJ

The Vortex is a large and dense student housing project. Does density bring many advantages to this realization in your opinion?

EV

I strongly defend the idea of the densification of construction that the Vortex represents as opposed to a series of smaller buildings with the same number of rooms. The exterior ramp replaces what would have been hallways that would have required heating and more lighting.

PJ

But why this defense of density on a fairly constrained site that is near sports fields and the forest?

EV

I am in favor of towers, of vertical construction. Demographic issues may not be an urgent problem in this area today, but they will be in 10 to 15 years. In the eight years since I became Architect of the Canton, it has gained 100,000 inhabitants. The solution is not to build where there is nothing, but to build onto the city, to densify. I am against making the territory non-homogeneous, for example by the scattered creation of urban centers in the place of agricultural land. We must remain in the urban centers that have already been built-up, and if we must densify, that means building vertically and making more use of public transport.

PJ

Why not build a tower in the place of the very large cylinder that was created?

EV

The large triangular area that forms the UNIL/EPFL complex is defined by the highway, a cantonal road, and a large avenue. The overall urban development of the area can be termed chaotic. When the French architect Dominique Perrault was a Professor at the EPFL he asked his students to work on the future of the site. His conclusions imagined 120-meter towers at each of the three points of the triangle. One of these towers has in fact been in the planning phase since 2015, when the Italian architect Stefano Boeri won a competition in Chavannes-près-Renens for a residential building covered with trees. The Vortex is nearly as high as it could be given local regulations, but the three towers imagined by Perrault would have been higher. The possibility of a tower for the student housing was not really taken into account, but a scheme like that of Perrault might be of interest in the future, both in terms of density and in order to better define the urban design of this important area for the universities of Lausanne.

PJ

Are you satisfied then with the Vortex as it was built?

EV

For me it is a source of immense pride. At the end of the competition, it was my task to present this project to the political authorities of the Canton, and in particular to Pascal Broulis, member of the Council of State and the head of Finance and External Relations. I carefully prepared my presentation, but I must admit that the nature of the competition and the choice of the project made me a bit worried. I showed him the plans and the model, but when it seemed to me that he was more interested in consulting his iPhone, I became even more concerned. When I finished my presentation, he put his iPhone in front of me and asked me if I knew of the Tulou villages in China (p. 16). The image on his phone closely resembled our model of the Vortex as seen from above. I had to admit that I was not familiar with these rather ancient structures.

“I strongly defend the idea of the densification of construction that the Vortex represents as opposed to a series of smaller buildings with the same number of rooms.” EV

And then he congratulated us and said: "It is a magnificent project." I believe that the Vortex, reaching back to this kind of historic reference, which was not in the mind of Jean-Pierre Dürig, remains an excellent example of how architecture can encourage people to live together. In July 2020, when the 829 available accommodations were first offered for rent, they were spoken for in less than 10 minutes online... an auspicious start. I hope that the students who live in the Vortex will look back favorably on their experience.[8]

Managing the Project

Pierre Eller, a private consultant with considerable experience in real estate, construction, and project management, sat down with the author to discuss his involvement in the Vortex project. Eller was one of the first participants to be signed on, working for the Canton of Vaud in 2014.

Philip Jodidio
What was the origin of the idea to build housing on the grounds of the University of Lausanne?

Pierre Eller
Because Lausanne is the Olympic Capital, the Mayor of the City (Syndic) Daniel Brélaz and Pascal Broulis, the head of the Finance Department of the Canton, were invited to the 2014 IOC Session. It seemed clear that Switzerland and Lausanne were not well placed to obtain the Summer or Winter Olympic Games, but that a candidacy for the 2020 Youth Olympic Games (YOG) might be a viable option. The Grand Council of Vaud voted a credit for studies in September 2014, and it was decided to launch an architectural competition for a signal project during the summer of 2015. Everybody knows that student housing in Lausanne poses difficulties, so it was decided to take a step toward resolving that question while also providing lodging for young athletes. A 30,000-square-meter plot of land that belonged to the Canton of Vaud was identified in the perimeter of the UNIL. For the YOG it was necessary to house 1,700 people. It was possible to put two athletes in each room whereas for university housing that number would be one. There was thus a need for 829 acommodations for students as well as some extra rooms for invited professors and university personnel, for example.

PJ
How did you become involved in the Vortex project?

PE
I received a mandate from the SIPaL (Service Immeubles, Patrimoine et Logistique, now called the DGIP) in July 2014 to help put together the program and competition for the housing project proposed in the context of the Lausanne 2020 Youth Olympic Games. We were also involved in the changes in the zoning plans of the University required by the new construction. This mandate ended in 2015, and thereafter, I continued to work beginning in 2016 on the project for the new owner, the Caisse de pensions de l'Etat de Vaud.

The first work meeting occurred in August 2014 and the competition was launched on October 31 of the same year. At that point, Lausanne had not yet been selected as the venue for the Games. Thirty-six architectural projects were submitted for the first round at the end of January 2015. The first jury selection was made on February 5-7, reducing the number of projects to seven, or rather six plus one.

PJ
Why do you refer to "six plus one," and what happened thereafter?

PE
Six of the projects were good but did not have what I would call a "brin de folie" (a touch of madness). The seventh project had been severely evaluated by a panel of experts before the competition and appeared to risk very high

8 Emmanuel Ventura in conversation with the author, Lausanne, September 24, 2020.

9 Pierre Eller in conversation with the author, Lausanne, September 29, 2020.

construction costs. The second-round projects were rendered at the end of April 2015, and the jury met again on May 21 and 22. Everybody was attracted to the Vortex project and it was chosen. I am an engineer and not an architect; for me, the idea of living together on a continuous street or a hive was very interesting.

PJ
You say that this is the first competition you have organized where the general contractor had a specific budget to respect. How did they manage to reduce costs while still respecting the architectural design? What is your impression of the final result?

PE
The basic strategy of the general contractor was to realize only what was strictly necessary for the project. They looked at what was planned for the basement, for example. Their competitors imagined a basement that ran along the full circumference of the circle. Lozinger Marazzi proposed to reduce the basements to two necessary areas, and in that way they saved six to eight million francs. The heating installation could thus be reduced in power and size as well. Another aspect of their optimization of the construction process was that the handrails were installed at the same time as the concrete ramp was being built. In that way, they avoided creating temporary handrails and scaffolding. I find that the Vortex is a success that is very close to the original concept. It was built on budget and on time.[9]

Great care was taken to respect the original design to the fullest extent possible. In an e-mail sent by the architect to the client on September 22, 2016, Jean-Pierre Dürig responded to a question about what the most important aspects of the design were—the elements that should definitely be retained. His response in five points is of interest. His five requests were:
1. Respect for the helicoidal spiral in rounded concrete (not faceted) with visible concrete ramp slabs.
2. The orthogonal geometry of the residential volumes.
3. The roof is to be publicly accessible and provide recreational activities; the counter-slope must be respected.
4. No built volumes in the interior courtyard.
5. Light and open railings.

From the University's Point of View

Benoît Frund is Vice-Rector of the University of Lausanne (UNIL), and was the person most closely associated with the Vortex project on the University side. As he explains, the construction of the Vortex represents a step toward resolving the long-standing issue of student housing for the Dorigny site, but it also marks a change of direction for the entire University, moving it closer to some foreign models that include housing on campus. Built beginning in the early 1970s, the Dorigny campus, which includes the EPFL, was not intended to function 24 hours a day, instead imagining that students, faculty, and personnel would be housed elsewhere. Since Dorigny is circumscribed by large roads and a rail line it is not easily penetrated as compared to other universities. Harvard in Cambridge, Massachusetts, for example, has dormitories on campus and is fully integrated into the town, whose commercial activity is in good part related to the University's community needs. The towns around the UNIL/EPFL campus are, instead, quite separate from it. According to Benoît Frund, the construction of the Vortex is a first significant step toward greater integration between the academic institution and its community.

Philip Jodidio
How did you become involved in the Vortex project, and what were some of the formal aspects of the relation of the project to the UNIL?

Benoît Frund
I am a member of the administration of the University in charge of Sustainability and the Campus; this concerns all new construction. In a formal sense, the overall University site

belongs to the Canton of Vaud. The University participates in new projects but is not the owner. In 2014, when Lausanne became a candidate for the 2020 Youth Olympic Games, the person in charge of the application, Denis Pitet, met with us on March 19, 2014, and said that the Canton had decided to use the Pala site, to build the Olympic Village to house athletes. An architectural competition was to be launched. We learned in that way that the Canton was taking a site that was destined to the development of the University. We are in the context of what is called the PAC 229 (Plan d'affectation Cantonal or Cantonal Allocation Plan), a document of the Canton which grants the development of the entire site to the universities (UNIL, EPFL, etc.). The existing PAC 229 had to be modified to allow for the construction of a residential building.

PJ
How did you approach the idea of new student housing on the grounds of the University?

BF
The mission of housing students is, in fact, in the hands of the FMEL. The UNIL was looking for ways to better house students, that is true. We were, however, thinking of building academic buildings on the site concerned. We of course agreed to the request of Mr. Pitet, but we said that we wanted to be closely associated with the project, in particular to be certain that the program included services that would be useful to the University. We obtained 76 apartments for visiting professors and other academic persons. We wanted a social component and there was a sports element in the program at the outset. There were sports facilities in the center of the Vortex originally, imagined by the architect to be below grade. These were eliminated for cost reasons essentially. We wanted space for student associations and a supplementary daycare facility. Since the image of the project was that of a village, we wanted a village hall, or social space, and we obtained that. In the completed project, aside from spaces for meetings and associations, there is a daycare center, a restaurant, a small store, and there will be a hairdresser.

PJ
What attracted you to the Vortex project during the jury deliberations?

BF
It was the idea of putting everyone under the same roof in a subtle way that attracted the entire jury. The original proposal of Dürig perhaps emphasized more clearly the idea of a continuous road in the form of a spiral ramp. There was a way of living together that was clearly inscribed in the project. The basic program was only to house a lot of people on a fairly small site—it was utilitarian. The Vortex project undertook to make the idea of living in a village a very particular one, which promised to be positive. The question was how to encourage people to actually live together, and that is the sense of our engagement for social spaces, for example. Although the use of the Vortex for the 2020 Youth Olympic Games was at a higher occupancy rate than normal, that period made it clear that the building does work the way we wanted it to.

PJ
What is your opinion of the Vortex as a piece of architecture in the context of the University?

BF
It immediately appeared that the Vortex might be considered as the iconic building of the University. However, that was not one of the objectives of the UNIL. The campus and the quality of its spaces and the coherence of the architecture were our real objectives. The site was originally a potato field with fairly mediocre characteristics for construction. I believe that the authorities felt that they could take this piece of land to house the Olympic athletes, but perhaps not on a more visible part of the campus. There was some concern and discussion about the cost reduction measures required, in particular the sports facilities in the courtyard that were removed. Since the Caisse

de pensions de l'Etat de Vaud was the actual client, we were, in fact, only the occupants of the building, but for a 25-year period, at least. The courtyard can still be more completely used in any case. There was a tent and a bistro in the central courtyard during the 2020 Youth Olympic Games. We imagined having a concert in the courtyard, but sound considerations make that difficult.

PJ
What role do you see the Vortex playing in the future of the University?

BF
This building clearly has an impact on the campus or rather on the overall site, which was originally intended to be filled with people in the morning and empty at night. The complex was not really conceived to be able to operate 24 hours a day with residents. The Vortex brings in residents where there were none before. This is a transition between a mono-functional site and a kind of small city. This is an occasion to share this presence with the neighboring town, for example. The actual town inhabitants rarely came into the campus unless they worked there. It is true that the campus is bordered by a train line, a highway, and a forest, which does isolate it to some extent. The Vortex creates a link where there was not one before. The campus does constitute a kind of urban park in an area that is quite developed otherwise, and then, too, I am convinced that the University must play a role in its community. The Vortex promises to open the University more to its urban environment.[10]

Bringing the Design to Fruition

The reasoning of the original architect of the Vortex, Jean-Pierre Dürig, is explained in the first section of this volume. Insofar as the finalization of the design and the supervision of the construction are concerned, Itten+Brechbühl, a large Swiss architectural firm with offices in Zurich, Basel, Bern, Lugano, and Lausanne, took the lead. Vincent Wolfensberger, an Associate Partner of the firm in Lausanne, was the project leader. In fact, Itten+Brechbühl at first worked for about six months at Dürig's side to speed up the planning process and then continued to work on the building in association with the general contractor, Losinger Marazzi, once Dürig had ended his collaboration. Wolfensberger explains: "We have experience in working with other architects, which may not be everyone's case, and we are familiar with the resolution of complex design and building issues. The idea of the very slightly inclined ramp and the residential boxes that had to be placed on it generated a degree of structural complexity that became urgent to resolve because of the upcoming Youth Olympic Games. We worked on preparing the invitation to tender and the diverse administrative filings required, as well as the invitation to tender for the general contractor. Our original mandate was completed at the same time as that of Jean-Pierre Dürig in 2016."

For the second phase, a competition was organized in which the general contractor was associated with an architect. For that phase, Itten+Brechbühl was coupled with Lozinger Marazzi. Wolfensberger continues: "We worked carefully on the areas of the building that were difficult or impossible to use in order to further rationalize the scheme. The idea was to reduce the overall volume while still fulfilling the program. We were able to use BIM (Building Information Modeling) for the project, which facilitated the management of changes on such a large scale. We were able, for example in a given stretch of the ramp, to increase from 11 to 12 the number of student rooms. We reduced the number of

10 Benoît Frund in conversation with the author, University of Lausanne, September 30, 2020.

"The Vortex promises to open the University more to its urban environment." BF

11 Vincent Wolfensberger, of Itten+Brechbühl, in conversation with the author September 29, 2020.

technical ducts as well. For budgetary reasons we reduced the width of exterior passageways. The overall impact of these changes was in some sense to shrink the building slightly and thus to reduce building costs." There were slight asymmetries in the ramps of the original design and those were smoothed out by the architects. They thus gained one and a half floors—about four meters in terms of the overall height of the building. Asked what he thinks of the final result, Vincent Wolfensberger responds: "I believe that the original idea of creating a village without any division has been carried forward in an optimal way, taking into account all of the architectural, construction, and cost issues posed. It remains what it was from the outset, a project that I would call nearly Utopian."[11] The task of Itten+Brechbühl was to carry forward a design that had already been laid out by Jean-Pierre Dürig at the same time as the firm "rationalized" certain aspects of the project, allowing it to be built on budget and on schedule.

Between Utopia and Reality

As has been made clear at the beginning of this volume, circles and spirals abound in nature and, indeed, in various aspects of culture throughout history. The cylinder has both the purity of modernity and ancient roots in the origins of geometry. The architect Jean-Pierre Dürig insists that his original design is neither a reference to nature nor to the history of architecture, where round or cylindrical buildings are frequent. What may, indeed, be unexpected is the combination of the inner spiral ramp and the outer cylindrical form, and yet the curvature of these two related elements makes them seem like a natural fit. As for the rejection of "natural" models, Dürig's own name for the Vortex assures that visitors will always have the image of a tornado or a whirlpool in mind when they visit. Nature and history are present even if they are rejected in a purely intellectual sense.

Dürig introduces another unexpected juxtaposition in his design, basing it entirely on curved forms and then inserting the actual dwelling units in an orthogonal pattern. This is what gives the Vortex its animated exterior and brings variety to the interior circumference. The spiraling ramp and the orthogonal arrangement of the apartments also clearly introduces complexity and difficulty to the design. Dürig says that he admires the International Style buildings of Mies van der Rohe and Gordon Bunshaft in New York, for example, where offices and interior spaces are essentially boxes inserted into a rigid, orthogonal frame. Dürig's take on this approach introduces a constraint—that of adapting a rectilinear housing system to a fundamentally curved building. Professing a dislike for façades, Dürig explains that in the case of the Vortex, it is the insertion of the wooden housing boxes that automatically generates the animated outer appearance of the building. The orthogonal order of Mies in America does seem to allow for little deviation from rectangular orthodoxy. Dürig seems to want to have it both ways, the curve and the box. His original drawings for the internal spiral admitted a certain number of irregularities that were duly removed for reasons of cost; still, such irregularity might be seen as being anathema to orthodox Modernism.

From Copenhagen to Moscow

Many of the main participants in the Vortex took the time to visit the Tietgenkollegiet student housing in Copenhagen (p. 31). This seven-story round building with 360 rooms was completed in 2006 by the architects Lundgaard & Tranberg. Here, the scale may be somewhat less daunting than the Vortex and a certain conviviality is exuded by the irregular wooden-clad housing units and the inner courtyard. All of the common areas are located in the courtyard, intentionally reinforcing the idea of community. Quite similar in many aspects to the Vortex, the Tietgenkollegiet is, however, designed as a set of stacked disks—

The architect Jean-Pierre Dürig insists that his original design is neither a reference to nature nor to the history of architecture, where round or cylindrical buildings are frequent.

there is no connecting spiral. The architects of the Tietgenkollegiet made explicit reference to the round Hakka or Tulou villages of southern China (p. 16), a reference that Jean-Pierre Dürig says he did not know about until Pascal Broulis drew it to his attention.

The Hakka people came from northern China to settle in the south. Beginning in the 17th century, because of conflict with neighboring people, they began to build easily defendable, usually round community living structures, also called Tulou, ranging in size up to 40,000 square meters. Although the primary motivation for the round form seems to have been defense, such structures clearly instill or translate a community spirit. Here too, there were no spiral ramps, so although they are analogous to the Vortex, the modern building is not precisely in the same mode.

The Bublik (p. 47) is a very large round apartment building located in the Ochakovo-Matveevskoe district of the Russian capital. It was in fact nicknamed Bublik (meaning "bagel" in Russian) because it resembles a bagel. With 26 entrances and 913 apartments and a repetitive façade design, the Bublik is usually termed "brutalist" in terms of design and, indeed, its massive size, with stacked, circular floors, does not immediately bring to mind the idea of conviviality. Nine stories high and 155 meters in diameter, the Bublik was completed in 1972 by the architect Eugene Stamo and the engineer Aleksandr Markelov. A total of three buildings of this type were completed by 1979, but further projects were abandoned due to what was declared to be excessive land use and construction costs that were higher than for a standard (rectangular) building.

It is interesting to note that despite his assertion that he has no historic references for the Vortex design, Jean-Pierre Dürig does point to the 97-meter-high Giralda Tower in Seville (completed in 1198 as the minaret of the Great Mosque of Seville) as an example. He looks there to the ramps that rise the full height of the tower through vaulted chambers arrayed around the structure's core. More revealing still, Dürig asserts that the idea of the Vortex "recalls that of the Soviets—all living together, something like Ivan Nikolaev's Communal House of the Textile Institute (Moscow, 1929–30, p. 151), which is a linear project. But for me, the Vortex is not a round building, it is linear." Built near Donskoy Monastery for students of the Textile Institute, the Communal House is a steel-frame structure with long ribbon windows that light 1,008 double sleeping cabins, each 2.3 × 2.7 meters in size. The building illustrates a radical approach to education and communal living that was popular in the early years of the Soviet Union. The early ideas of Le Corbusier and his book *Vers une architecture* (1923), where he wrote "La maison est une machine à habiter" (A house is a machine for living in) had a direct influence on Constructivism in the Soviet Union, of which the Communal House is a seminal example. It may be interesting to note that Le Corbusier's only built structure in Moscow, the very large Tsentrosoyuz Building (1933), relied specifically on ramps. The Swiss-French architect stated: "We have approached the problem as urban planners, that is, we have considered that corridors and stairs are, so to speak, enclosed streets. In consequence, these streets are 3.25 meters wide, and are always well lit. Moreover, we have replaced tiring flights of stairs with gently sloping (14%) ramps that allow for free and easy circulation."[12] Dürig's reference to the Communal House and Le Corbusier's comment on his own Tsentrosoyuz Building bring together references to modern architecture that point the way to a "linear" building (albeit a circular one) that makes extensive use of ramps in the image of urban planning. Dürig speaks of the *strassendorf* villages organized around a single street. It is only necessary to imagine wrapping such a street around a cylinder to grasp the architect's thought process. Although rooms in the Vortex have an area between 15 and 22 square meters as opposed to the six square meters proposed in double occupancy in the Textile Institute building, the idea of communal living remains.

12 Le Corbusier, quoted in Jean-Louis Cohen's book *Le Corbusier and the Mystique of the USSR: Theories and Projects for Moscow, 1928–1936*, Princeton University Press, 1992.

Immanent Geometry

As their remarks reveal, the participants in the jury for the Vortex were all attracted to the idea of students living in a continuous village, whose connections are made manifest by the 2.8-kilometer ramp that links the levels of the building. Both Emmanuel Ventura and Vincent Wolfensberger refer to a utopian project. In this way the concept of "living together" forms the sociological equivalent of the immanent nature of Dürig's spiral inscribed in a circle. The word *immanent* has two related definitions:
- existing or operating within; inherent;
- (of God) permanently pervading and sustaining the universe.

It has been underlined here that even in the face of the architect's insistence that the Vortex design is unrelated to natural circles or spirals, it is clear that these forms pervade the universe. Architectural, artistic, and cultural references follow the same logic. In short, a building that derives from the templates of nature and concepts of modern architectural design is meant to serve the utopian purpose of bringing people together in a spiral village.

The Vortex seems to be an expression of architectural rigor, a perfect spiral inscribed in a perfect circle, and yet there are many elements that have come into play to create this image. Jean-Pierre Dürig himself stated to the jury President that this building was not meant to be built; it was paper architecture, an informed flight of fantasy, a utopian dream. And yet the project won the competition and was built. That transition from dream to reality was, of course, in part the work of the original architect, but it was also the fruit of considerable efforts undertaken by all concerned; those who have expressed themselves here and many others. Pragmatism, realism, and extensive knowledge of architecture and engineering were required to turn Dürig's original drawings into concrete, wood, and glass. Some have found that the scale of the building may belie its village-like origin, but the ideas of continuity and living together certainly survived the inevitable process of economic and structural rationalization. Neither the architect nor, indeed, the University where the Vortex is located sought to create an emblematic presence. Rather, they were interested in the first instance in finding the best solution to a complex architectural problem, and in the second in finding an efficient way to solve housing problems. And yet, both candidly admit that the Vortex has imposed itself as an "iconic" presence. And it is iconic because it is so clearly based on fundamental forms, because it represents a real effort to bring people together in a democratic and responsible way. Whether the village-like atmosphere devoutly hoped for will materialize in the long term remains to be seen, but in a relatively discreet site, Lausanne and its University have honored the real sense of architecture.

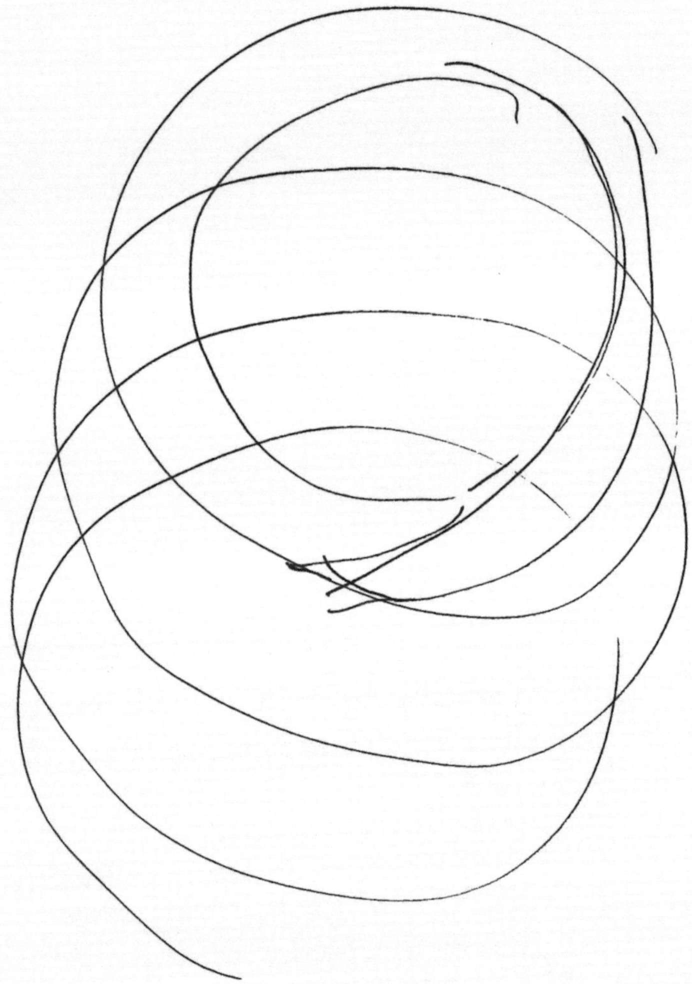

The designer of the Vortex is Jean-Pierre Dürig, a Zurich-based architect who is committed to a form of Modernism that allows for structural surprises, such as the 2.8-kilometer-long ramp that marks the interior circumference of the Vortex. He discussed his design and the project with the author in his office in Zurich.

Philip Jodidio
How did you come to be interested enough in the Lausanne project to submit a competition entry?

Jean-Pierre Dürig
I enter 20 competitions or more each year. In a way, it is not 20 projects a year you do, it is one, and one influences the other. You think simultaneously about 10 different projects. This was an open competition, the site was beautiful, and the program was absolutely spectacular: to create 800 rooms for a thousand people. The site was just grassland, with a graveyard and sports fields nearby, and forest. It was virgin in a way, not pre-conditioned by other nearby structures. Here, because the program was so strong, we had to go to the basics. Normally, you have alignments and neighbors to deal with, and here that was not the case. But we did have to keep the building under a height of 30 meters so as not to fall under high-rise legislation, which imposes stringent conditions for fire and exits for example. And then, it is not a site for a high-rise.

PJ
What are some of the underlying concepts of your competition entry? Where does the name Vortex come from?

J-PD
We went very close to the height limit. At the end of the spiral walk, you should see the lake. In a way, once we had the idea, it was easy to fit the design into the irregular but basically square site. I wanted to create a neighbor for the forest that would not have strong edges. The main idea for the building comes from the program, which indicated the number of rooms and the number of students. The idea is that you are not living in a house but, instead, on a long road. It is like the villages we call *strassendorf* (street villages). There are villages that are centered on a square or a church and then there are villages that form along a street. Here, every student lives along a single two-kilometer path that is a spiral. The name "Vortex" was ours and was the idea of my collaborator Verena Nelles. We gave it this name after handing in the competition documents.

We learned later that the building would also be the Olympic Village for the Lausanne 2020 Youth Olympic Games. Here nobody lives apart, everyone is part of the entire society constituted by the Vortex. I didn't want the students to live in different buildings or houses but to live all together, along the lines of Le Corbusier's Unité d'Habitation (for example the Cité Radieuse, Marseille, 1952, p. 151). The overall form is round because it was the easiest geometric form to fit into the site. Something with freer curves would have been too "fashionable" and it would not have been understandable in the midst of a big field. The outside of the building is a perfect circle but, at the time of the competition, the inner circumference was not a perfect shape because of the different sizes of the units. But we had to resolve this and create a circle along the inner surface as well for reasons of construction costs.

PJ
Did you have in mind references to other round buildings that exist in the world?

J-PD
Pascal Broulis brought up the fact that in China there are round residential buildings called Tulou or Hakka villages (p. 16). We were not aware of that. We had in mind a very open, very democratic building. Our references were not historic, but instead functional and were based on an idea of how students should live together.

Part of an original sketch by Jean-Pierre Dürig showing the spiral ramp of the Vortex.

The typology of round or spiral buildings like the Guggenheim (p. 34) in New York were not part of our thought process; instead, it was about how we could bring people together in an architectonic way. Normally in round buildings, the apartments would be arranged along the radius, but we imagined them according to an orthogonal grid. We wanted to differentiate the units instead of creating a smooth exterior façade. A radial solution would make a single, smooth building, but here the boxes that form the apartments are like houses on the road or in this case a path. The apartments are like little buildings. The continuous path makes it easier to go up within the overall circular form. Inside the thick walls of the Giralda Tower (1198), which was built as the minaret of the Great Mosque of Seville before becoming the bell tower of the Cathedral, there are also inclined ramps. We imagined an iconic building that would be part of the extended UNIL/EPFL campus. At the top of the spiral, you would see the lake and the Alps. We imagined a café at the upper end of the ramp to invite the students to go up.

PJ
Might it not have been simpler to have visible structural supports for the interior access ramp? What is the reason for avoiding that solution?

J-PD
The structure that supports the ramps is inside the building; there are no visible columns and that gives an impression of a floating path going upward. This makes the building appear to be light. If the supporting structure were on the inside of the ramp, you would see the building first; instead, you see the path. The circular form means that there are two directions of view: one from the apartments looking out and the other from the ramps looking in. The inner diameter and thus the central space is 105 meters across. It is a very important space for the campus. If there is activity in the inner courtyard, that is part of the concept; you all live together. The idea recalls that of the Soviets—all living together, something like Ivan Nikolaev's Communal House of the Textile Institute (Moscow, 1929–30), which is a linear project. For me, the Vortex is not a round building, it is linear.

PJ
Round forms of course exist in architecture but they are also very present in nature. Was that part of your thought process?

J-PD
As an architect, I feel that we have to work with nature, but that we have to do the opposite. You can't copy nature, that is not possible. Architecture is something artificial. You have to respect nature with considerations of sunlight, wind, and ecology, but the form of an architectural structure should be totally abstract. We solved the problem with minimal, geometric means. It is a programmatic decision and then it is a geometric decision, but there are no references or symbolism. But if people make such associations with this building, it is fine with me. A work of art can always be interpreted. Different people see different things. The more different interpretations there are, the better the building is. I am still a modest maker of structures. I don't even consider myself to be a creative architect; I want to resolve problems in a clear, simple, good way. The cylindrical form was in no way the goal; it was a question of how the program could be resolved on this site in the simplest, most functional way.

PJ
Did you have some concern that the design and in particular the ramp might be too expensive to build?

J-PD
The proof that it was a cost-effective solution was that they found an investor who wanted to get his money back. The Caisse de pensions (CPEV) would never have invested in it if it were an extravagant project. Maybe it could have been cheaper if it had been built in a more traditional, or lower way. It is wonderful that you have a client who wants to create more than rooms. We considered many different schemes, rectangular or in different buildings, but we were not

↗ Le Corbusier, façade of the Cité Radieuse, Marseille, France, 1952.

→ Ivan Nikolaev, Communal House of the Textile Institute, Moscow, 1929–30, drawing.

convinced because we did not find what made it special for a thousand students. Don't tell anybody, but if you enter a competition you try to go in as powerfully as possible as an architect and hope that the costs will work out. And the costs come back at you when you have to build; you have to make it more regular, rational, and dense, but we did not lose the main concept. There is still the geometry, the ramp, and the idea of living together. We managed to put every room in the building that the program required.

PJ
What are some of your architectural references—figures you admire in the past or even the present?

J-PD
I am inspired by many architects, but when it comes to designing, you are alone with geometry, program, and functionality. I have a modern base in my work, but I started in Post-Modernism between 1980 and 1985. When I completed the EPFZ, I worked with Ernst Gisel and that helped me a lot and then I had to go back in my thought process through to Mies van der Rohe. I think of Gordon Bunshaft and SOM in the 1960s and Mies in America and their strong flexible structures. The architects of the International Style had what I would call a scientific-functional approach, expressed in accordance with a minimal, sober expression that remains timeless. Architecture in their hands was seen as a superordinate social and cultural system and not as a personal expression of one's state of mind.

PJ
Did Mies and Bunshaft have some intellectual impact on your design for the Vortex?

J-PD
Their work was interesting to me because there were essentially no façades. The surface was a function of the structure—you put the boxes in and that was it. I hate designing façades. The façade is generated by the floors and the line of boxes. No façade, that is what I understand architecture is—structure, program, and function. I also do buildings where you can see the structure but using columns for the visible parts of the Vortex would have been in contradiction with the idea of the path progressing upward with huts or cabins along the way. This concept meant that I could not use architectonic elements in the façade.

PJ
Do you recognize that the Vortex is a kind of iconic building?

J-PD
The goal was not to make something different than what people have seen. The goal was to make it perfect for the program, the students, and the site. I like the way it looks, and I recognize that it is iconic, but that was not the goal. I also designed the curved and split bridge that connects all traffic to and from the Vortex in one swing. The bridge was part of the competition, and we worked with the engineers Muttoni & Fernandez from Lausanne.[13]

13 Jean-Pierre Dürig in conversation with the author, Zurich, July 18, 2019.

Jean-Pierre Dürig, sketches of the Passerelle de la Sorge bridge leading to the Vortex.

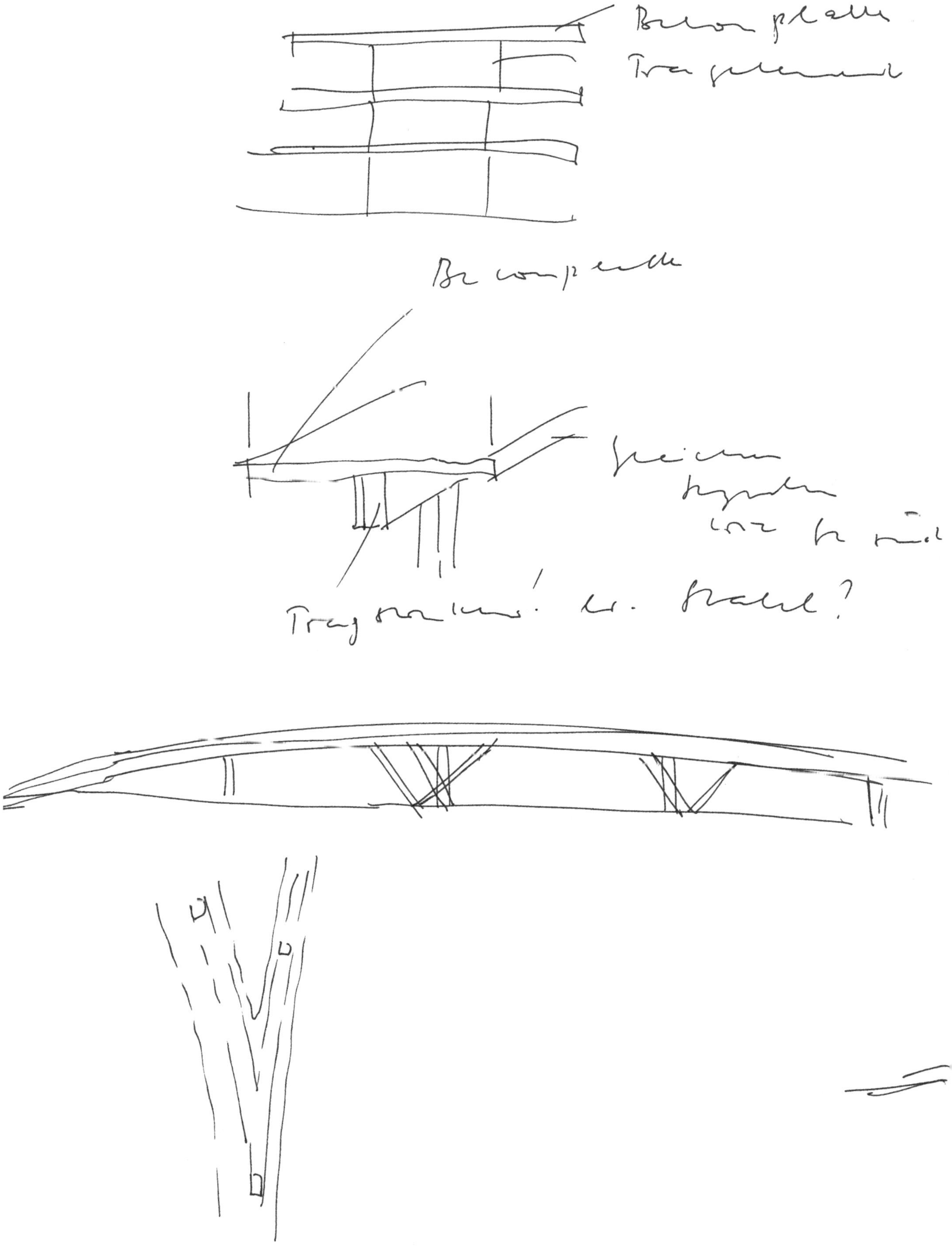

03.07.15 Chavannes Brücke

A CONSISTENT AND IDEALISTIC ATTITUDE

Born in Winterthur, Switzerland, in 1958, Jean-Pierre Dürig studied architecture at the EPFZ in Zurich (1979–85). From 1982 to 1987, he worked in the office of the respected architect Ernst Gisel. Between 1987 and 1989, Dürig created his own architectural office in Zurich, an initiative that was succeeded by Dürig & Rämi architects (1990–2002). Since 2003, he has been at the head of Dürig AG. He has taught at EPFZ (1996–98) and at the Architecture Academy in Mendrisio (2004–06). Competitions play an important role for Dürig AG. According to the office: "They are not only the basis for building contracts, but also, nationally and internationally, the motor for the creative potential of the office." The office focuses on public and infrastructure buildings, which often involve unusual construction tasks or programs. This was certainly the case of the Vortex project, but also for what may be Jean-Pierre Dürig's most visible project, his complete restructuring of the main railway station of Zurich (2002–13) with the design of an underground station. They have also completed a school located above a bus depot (SA Wetzikon Schellerareal), and a design concept for a new administrative city in South Korea (2005).

According to the reasoning presented by the architect's office: "Dürig AG is looking for superordinate connections on a large scale. It understands form as a means to make the society, the building, or the city function. Nevertheless, it responds strategically with very strong, radical forms that sharpen the readability of the concept. The goal is a consistent and idealistic attitude in order to be robust against the complex influences that can break a concept. The result is a generosity and simplicity that is often emblematic." In his efforts to advance after winning the Vortex project, Dürig made it clear that he was not eager to substantially reduce the cost of his proposal. This might be seen as being "robust against the complex influences that can break a concept," but in dealing with an essentially public project, it is clear from the outset that budgets are not readily extendable.

In parallel with the Vortex project, Jean-Pierre Dürig designed the curved and split bridge that serves the site of the housing complex (Passerelle de la Sorge). It was completed in 2018 in collaboration with the engineers Muttoni & Fernandez. Part of the original competition, the bridge served during the final construction process for the Vortex and now serves for pedestrians and cyclists connecting Chavannes with the University campus and the Vortex. As the architect says: "The organic routing directly connects geometries, places, and functions."

Jean-Pierre Dürig is clearly interested in the fundamentals of architectural design, participating in numerous competitions that require an intelligent and complete analysis of complex projects and programs. His approach is carefully thought-out and strictly reasoned in terms of his own appreciation of architecture. Influenced by Modernist thinking and realizations, he nonetheless goes further than earlier conceptualizations in order to create radical designs that maintain an appearance of calm, rational, and apparently simple solutions.

Jean-Pierre Dürig, the Passerelle de la Sorge bridge with the Vortex in the background.

Total volume
121,030 m³

Site area
30,447 m²

Built area
6,110 m²

Exterior diameter
137 m

Interior diameter
105 m

Height
27 m

Length of spiral ramp
2.8 kilometers

Bedrooms
941

Residents approximately
1,000

↗ Site plan
→ Section

0
10
20
30

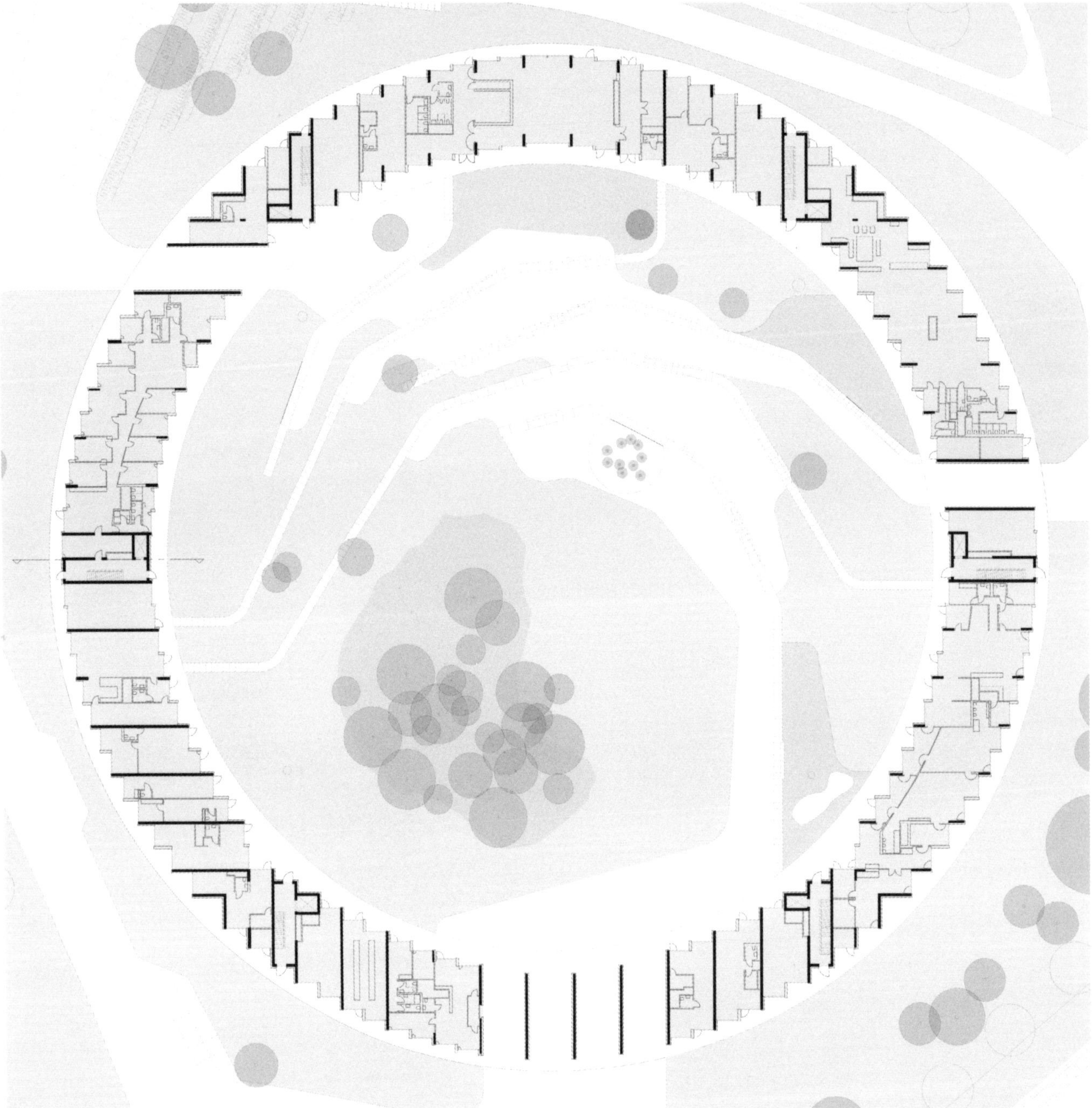

Ground floor

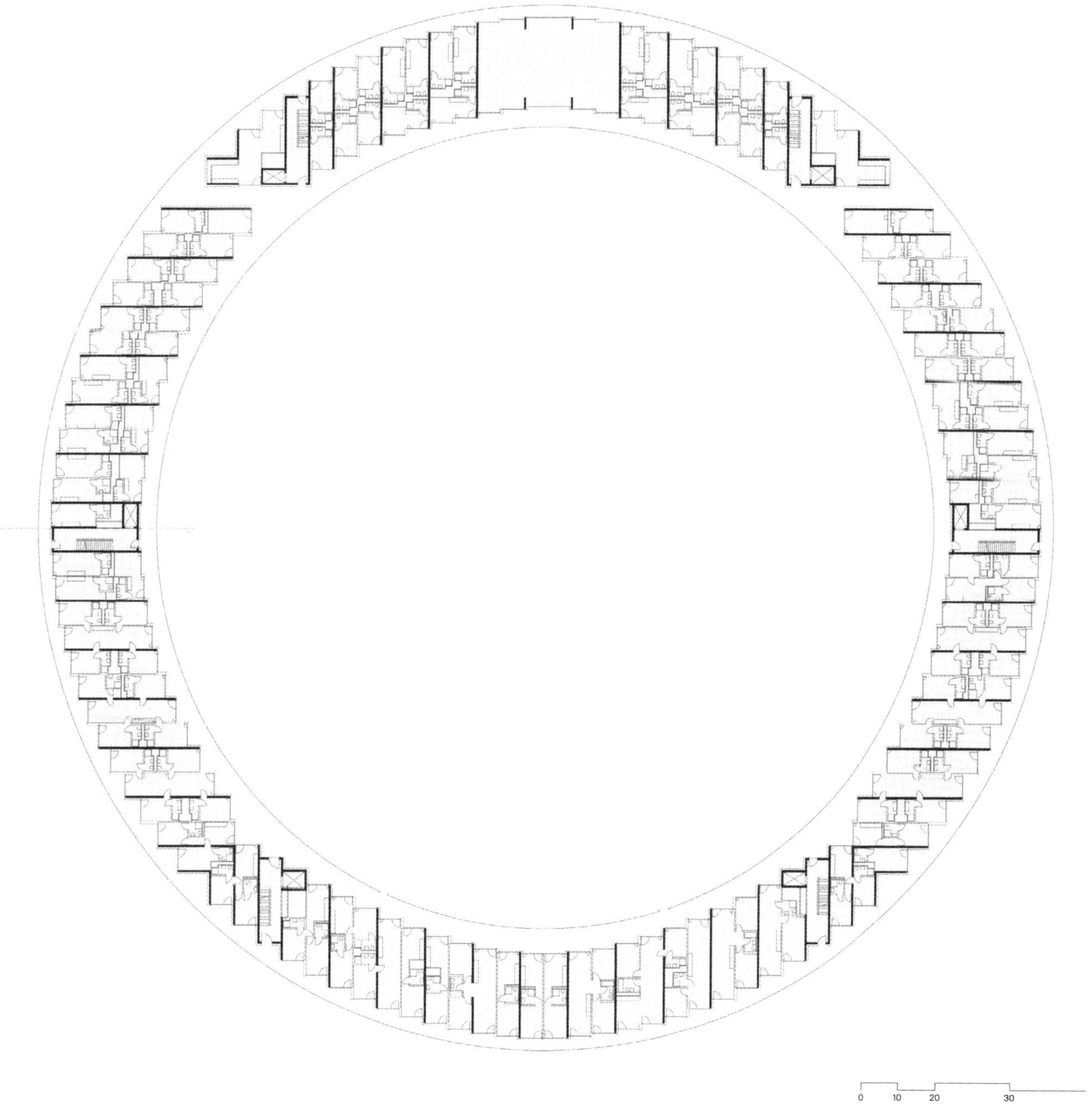

Level 1

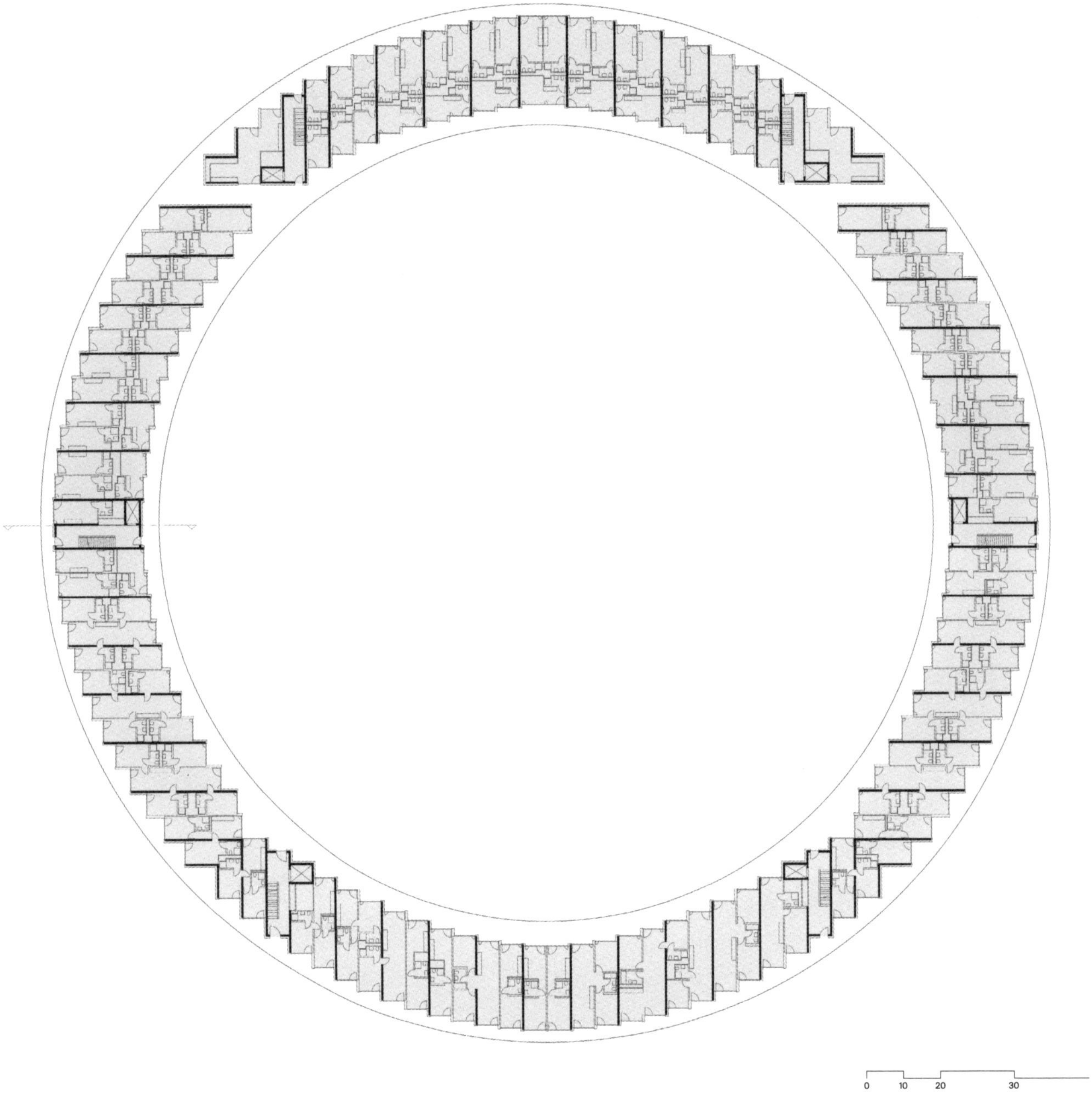

Levels 2–3

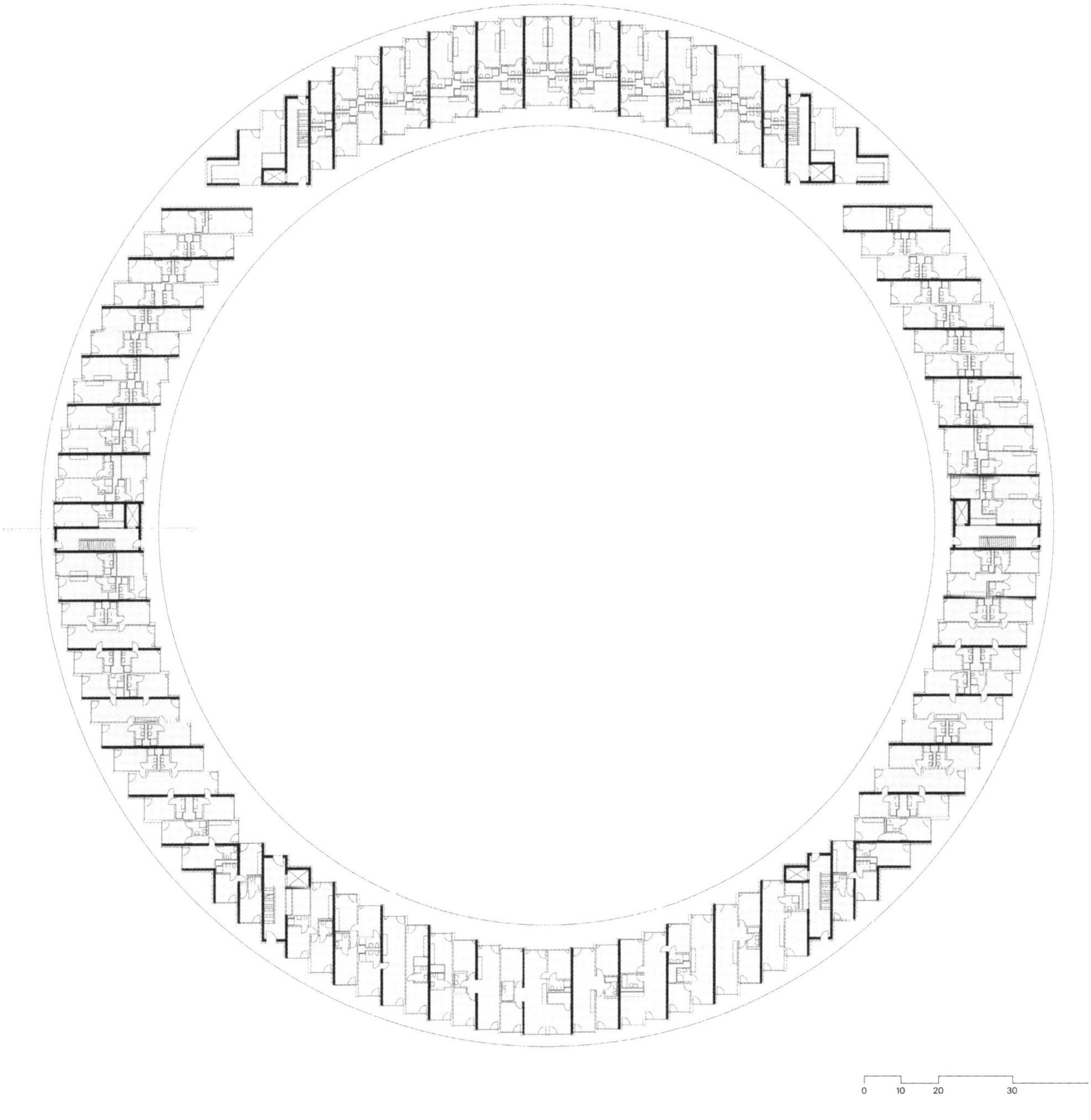

Levels 4–7

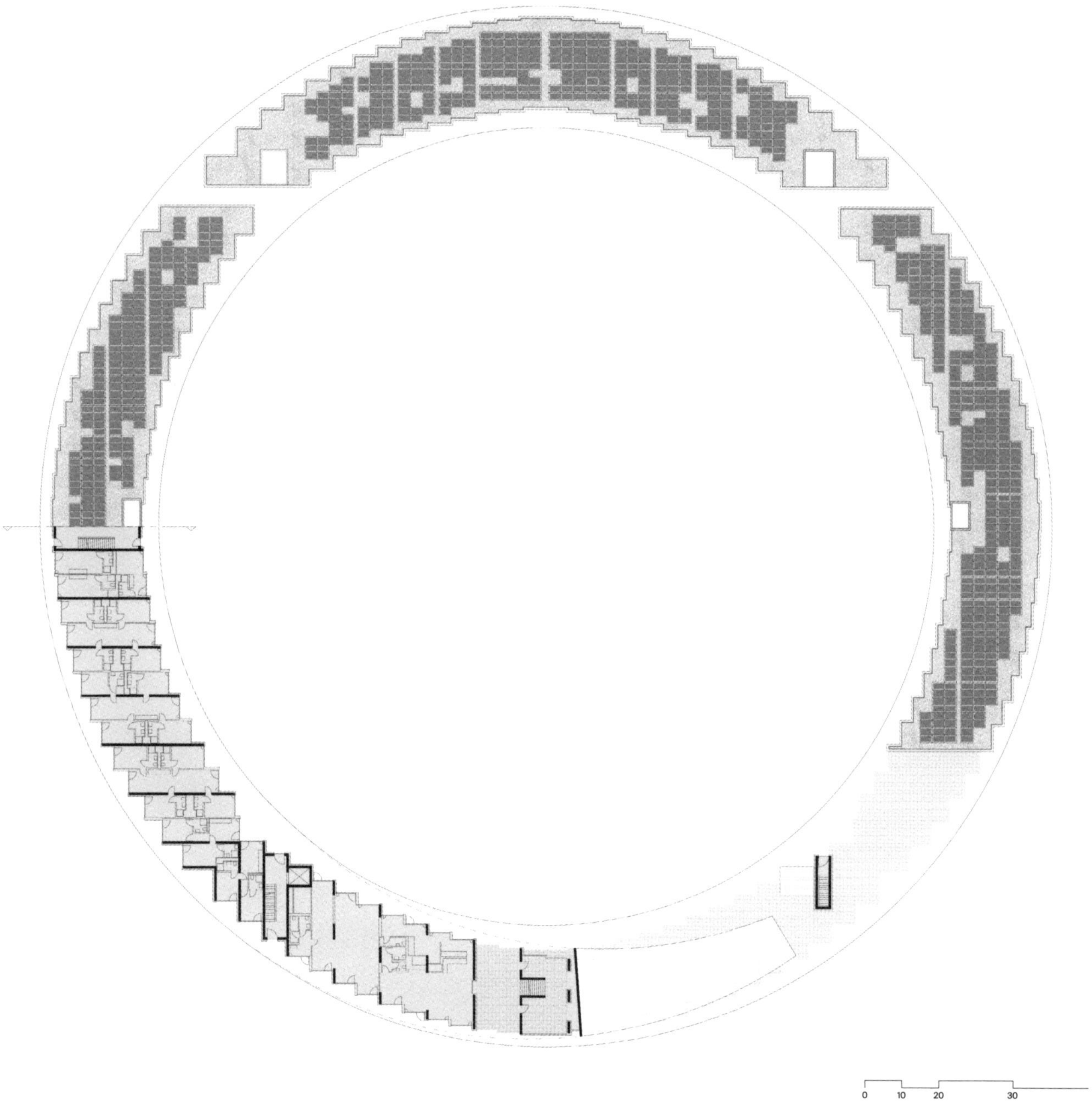

Level 8

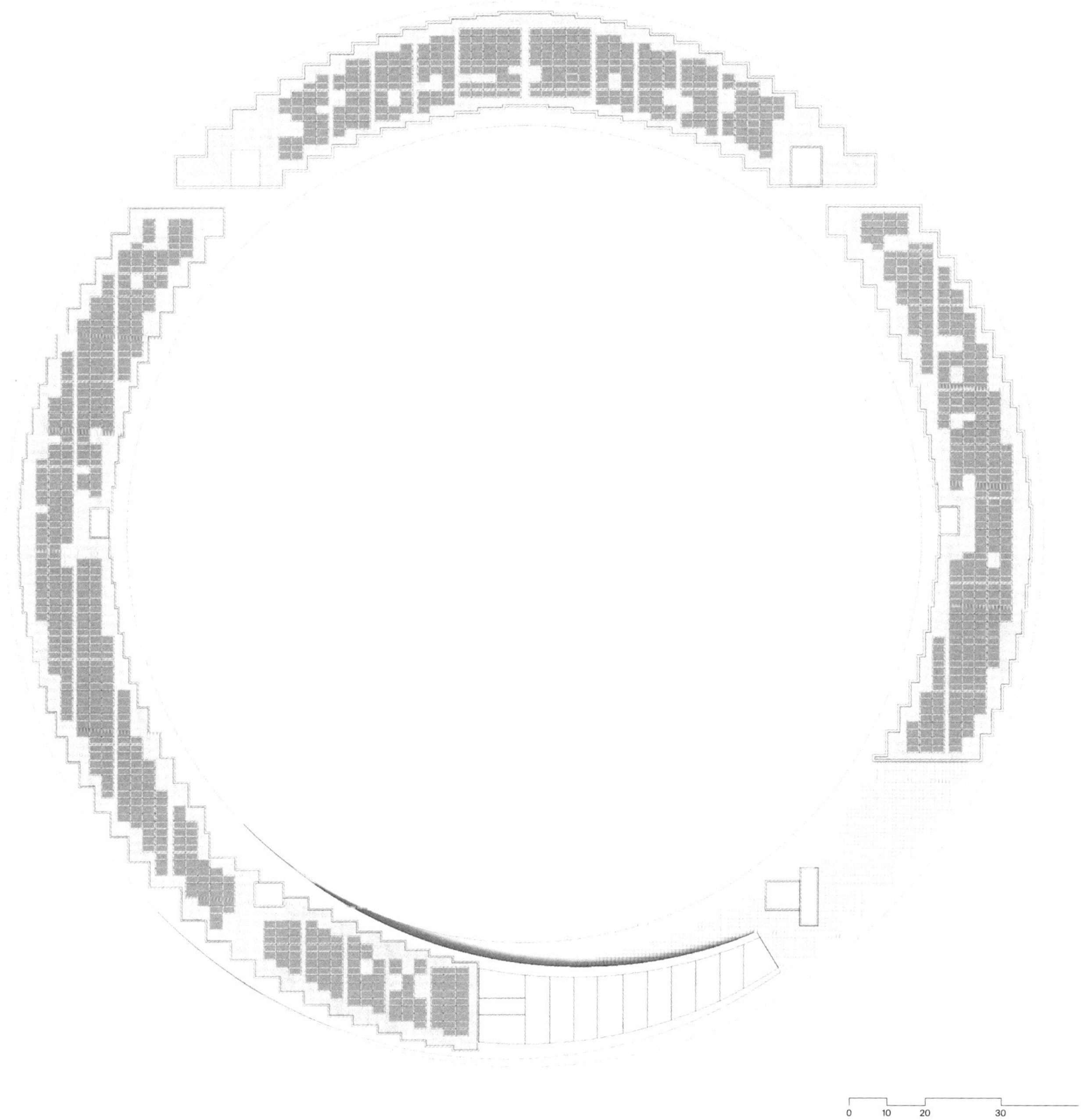

Roof

ACKNOWLEDGMENTS

Development phase, preliminary studies, architectural competition, first draft, final draft, public enquiry:

1. Client
État de Vaud
Département des finances et des relations extérieures (DFIRE)
Direction générale des immeubles et du patrimoine (DGIP)
Direction de l'architecture et de l'ingénierie (DAI)
Pascal Broulis
Philippe Pont
Emmanuel Ventura
Olivier Andreotti
Fabiano Bianchetti
Pierre Eller

2. Contributor State services
Christian Exquis
Pascale Pacozzi
Pierre Bays

3. Competition jury
Emmanuel Ventura
Philippe Pont
Chantal Ostorero
Dominique Arlettaz
Philippe Cardinaux
André Gorgerat
François Guichon
Denis Pittet
Michel Staffoni
Jean-Gilles Décosterd
Olivier Fazan
Eric Frei
Patrick Heiz
Martin Bornand
Yves Roulet
Pascale Pacozzi
Julie Pollard
Greg Curchod
Claude Daetwyler
Benoît Frund
Alain Lapaire
Fabiano Bianchetti
Célien Devaux
Pierre Gerster
Patrick Arnold
Vincent Krayenbühl
Patrick Rérat
Aurélie Potocki
Olivier Andreotti
Manuel Bauer
Pierre Bays
Pierre Eller
Xavier Fischer
Bernard Flach
Kevin Forestier
Patric Frei
Wolfgang Martz
Alain Oulevey
Jacques-André Vulliet

4. Winning architects and agents
Jean-Pierre Dürig
Studio Vulkan
MWV Bauingenieure AG
Amstein + Walthert
Befair AG
Itten+Brechbühl
Muttoni et Fernández
De Cérenville
Abplanalp Affolter Partner
Pirmin Jung
Préface Sàrl

5. Direction générale de l'enseignement supérieur (DGES)
Chantal Ostorero
Pierre de Almeida

6. University of Lausanne (UNIL)
Dominique Arlettaz
Nouria Hernandez
Benoît Frund
Ruben Merino
Yann Jeannin

Request for proposals and realization:

7. Board of Directors
Christian Budry †
Stephen Sola
Michèle Mottu Stella
Gloria Capt
Michel Berney
Fabrice Ghelfi
Yves Froidevaux
Alain Martin
Alexandre Bernel
Jean Daniel Martin

8. CPEV Real Estate Investment Committee

Michel Berney

Gloria Capt

9. Steering committee

Philippe Pont

Emmanuel Ventura

Chantal Ostorero

Benoît Frund

Alain Lapaire

Philippe Cardinaux

Sébastien Henchoz

Thierry Pelichet

Pierre Eller

Frederik Flaccomio

Élodie Tovaglieri

Florence Klarer

10. Youth Olympic Games (YOG)

Virginie Faivre

Ian Logan

Patrick Stalder

Patrick Baumann †

Sébastien Dauxerre

Cédric Destraz

Alistair Davidson

Jérôme Rochat

Lise Cordey

Caterina Piovano

11. University of Lausanne (UNIL)

Nouria Hernandez

Benoît Frund

Ruben Merino

Yann Jeannin

Julien Meillard

Géraldine Falbriard

Philippe Gagnebin

Alain Dayer

Augustin Fragnière

12. Fondation Maison pour étudiants Lausanne (FMEL)

Chantal Ostorero

François Guichon

Pierre de Almeida

Alexandre Dayer

Eric Grande

13. Retraites Populaires (RP)

Eric Birchmeier

Nicole Samuel-Manzo

Yves-Marie Hostettler

Philippe Doffey

Alain Pahud

Lorraine Clément

Véronique Dénéreaz

Alain Lapaire

Sébastien Henchoz

Thierry Pelichet

Frederik Flaccomio

Stefano Lepri

Claudia Alves

Sophie Gonin

Daniel Kiani

Anne Dietrich

Philippe Vauthey

Élodie Tovaglieri

Florence Klarer

14. GO opérationnel

Frederik Flaccomio

Élodie Tovaglieri

Pierre Eller

Roland Linzaghi

Éric Burg

Charles Mialon

Nicolas Asper

Benoît Demarle

Didier Simongiovanni

Vincent Wolfensberger

Guillaume Schobinger

15. Losinger Marazzi total company and agents

Pascal Bärtschi

Christophe Lirot

Éric Burg

Charles Mialon

Nicolas Asper

Benoît Demarle

Didier Simongiovanni

Tecnoservice Engineering SA

Perrin – Spaeth SA

Baertschi Ingénieurs SA

Impact-Concept SA

Ignis Salutem SA

Itten+Brechbühl

Thomas Jundt SA

Maître Carré Sàrl

PPLUS Sàrl

Renaud et Burnand SA

16. École hôtelière de Lausanne (EHL)

Michel Rochat

René Wallbaum

CREDITS

Cover © Fernando Guerra, Itten+Brechbühl SA
p. 14 Gift of the Friends of the Institute's Teahouse Fund / Bridgeman Images
p. 15 CaptureAndCompose / Adobe Stock
p. 16 rabbit75_fot / Adobe Stock
p. 17 Christie's Images / Bridgeman Images
p. 18 lucapost / flickr / CC BY-NC-ND 2.0
p. 19 scaliger / Adobe Stock
p. 20 Photo 12 / Alamy Stock Photo
p. 21 © Bibliothèque nationale de Russie Saint-Pétersbourg
p. 22 World History Archive / Alamy Stock Photo
p. 23 Massimo Merlini / iStock Photo
p. 24 © 2021, ProLitteris, Zurich. Photo Bridgeman Images
p. 25 IMAGO / ZUMA Wire
p. 26 Elementalimaging / iStock Photo
p. 27 Department of Culture and Tourism - Abu Dhabi / Photo Hufton+Crow
p. 28 Reciprocity Images / Stockimo / Alamy Stock Photo
p. 29 Fondation Beyeler, Riehen / Basel
© 2021 ProLitteris, Zurich. Photo: akg-images
p. 30 akg-images
p. 31 Jens Lindhe, Copenhagen
p. 32 INTERFOTO / Alamy Stock Photo
p. 33 World History Archive / Alamy Stock Photo
p. 34 Inge Johnsson / Alamy Stock Photo
p. 35 © 2021, ProLitteris, Zurich. Photo bpk / Städel Museum
p. 36 bilwissedition Ltd. & Co. KG / Alamy Stock Photo
p. 37 © 2021, ProLitteris, Zurich.
Photo Cavan Images / Alamy Stock Photo
p. 38 The Natural History Museum / Alamy Stock Photo
p. 39 NASA / GSFC / Arizona State University
p. 40 AF Fotografie / Alamy Stock Photo
p. 41 Martin Berry / Alamy Stock Photo
p. 42 © 2021, ProLitteris, Zurich. Photo Martin Shields / Alamy Stock Photo
p. 43 Nacasa & Partners Inc.
p. 44 IMAGO / ZUMA Wire
p. 45 Science History Images / Alamy Stock Photo
p. 46 F. Fox / blickwinkel
p. 47 Kosmaj / Shutterstock
p. 48 daliu / Adobe Stock
p. 49 Johan Gjøde - Aarhus / Billeder
p. 50 FineArt / Alamy Stock Photo
p. 51 © Fernando Guerra, Itten+Brechbühl SA
p. 54 © Dürig AG architectes
p. 56 © MHL
pp. 58–59 © SAUL
pp. 60–61 © UNIL
pp. 63, 64, 65, 66–67, 68, 73
© Losinger Marazzi / Benoît Demarle
pp. 70–71, 72 © Michel Berney
pp. 75–77 © Christiane Nill
pp. 78, 80, 81, 83, 84–85, 87, 88, 89, 90, 91
92, 93, 94 © Fernando Guerra, Itten+Brechbühl SA
pp. 98–99, 101, 102–103, 105, 106–107, 108–109, 111, 112–113, 114–115, 116–117, 118–119 © Matthieu Gafsou
pp. 120–121, 122–123 © Mathieu Bernard-Reymond
pp. 126, 130 © Dürig AG architectes
pp. 134, 137, 138, 141, 143, 144–145, 146–147
© Fernando Guerra, Itten+Brechbühl SA
pp. 148, 153 © Dürig AG architectes
p. 151 Berlin-Zeitgeist / Alamy Stock Photo
p. 155 © Ruedi Walti, Basel
pp. 157–163 © Itten+Brechbühl SA
p. 167 © Mathieu Bernard-Reymond
Back cover © Dürig AG architectes

VORTEX
ARCHITECTURE OF THE CIRCLE

First published in the United States
of America in 2021 by
Rizzoli International Publications, Inc.
300 Park Avenue South
New York, NY 10010
www.rizzoliusa.com

Texts
Philip Jodidio
Forewords
Michel Berney
Pascal Broulis

Publisher
Charles Miers
Editorial Director
Catherine Bonifassi
Art Direction
Atelier Cocchi, Lausanne
Flavia Cocchi, Christine Vaudois
Picture Editor
Beatrice Geistlich, Zurich
Editor
Victorine Lamothe
Production Director
Maria Pia Gramaglia
Production Manager
Kaija Markoe
Managing Editor
Lynn Scrabis

Editorial Coordination
CASSI EDITION
Vanessa Blondel
Lili Doillon
Harriet Graham
Abigail Grater

ISBN: 978-0-8478-6953-4
Library of Congress Control Number: 2021934563
2021 2022 2023 2024 / 10 9 8 7 6 5 4 3 2 1
Printed in Italy

Visit us online:
Facebook.com/RizzoliNewYork
Twitter: @Rizzoli_Books
Instagram.com/RizzoliBooks
Pinterest.com/RizzoliBooks
Youtube.com/RizzoliNY
Issuu.com/Rizzoli